Autism & PDD™ Concept De
Clothing

by Pam Britton Reese and Nena C. Challenner

Skills

- concept development
- language

Ages

- 3 through 8

Grades

- PreK through 3

Evidence-Based Practice

- Early intervention that addresses skill acquisition in the areas of interaction, attention, play, comprehension, and expression will support the development of an even profile. The acquisition of key developmental skills supports the later development of communication, language, and speech and enhances emotional, social, and academic development (RCSLT, 2005).

- Many children with autism spectrum disorders learn more readily through the visual modality (RCSLT, 2005).

- Students need to understand semantic connections among words for academic success (NRP, 2000).

- Vocabulary intervention should provide opportunities for students to use target words in multiple contexts (Boone et al., 2007).

Autism & PDD Concept Development: Clothing incorporates these principles and is also based on expert professional practice.

References

Boone, K., Letsky, S., Wallach, S., Young, J., Gingrass, K., & Daly, C. (2007, November 28). *Role of SLP: A method of inclusion.* Paper presented at the 2007 ASHA National Convention. Retrieved March 24, 2009 from http://convention.asha.org/2007/handouts/1137_1371Letsky_Sarah__107277_Nov28_2007_Time_071812AM.ppt

National Reading Panel (NRP). (2000). *Teaching children to read: An evidence-based assessment of the scientific research literature on reading and its implications for reading instruction—Reports of the subgroups.* Retrieved March 24, 2009 from www.nichd.nih.gov/publications/nrp/upload/report.pdf

Royal College of Speech & Language Therapists (RCSLT). (2005). *Clinical guidelines for speech and language therapists.* Retrieved March 24, 2009 from www.rcslt.org/resources/clinicalguidelines

LinguiSystems®

LinguiSystems, Inc.
3100 4th Avenue
East Moline, IL 61244
800-776-4332

FAX: 800-577-4555
Email: service@linguisystems.com
Web: linguisystems.com

Copyright © 2001 LinguiSystems, Inc.

All of our products are copyrighted to protect the fine work of our authors. You may only copy the student materials as needed for your own use. Any other reproduction or distribution of the pages in this book is prohibited, including copying the entire book to use as another primary source or "master" copy.

Printed in the U.S.A.

ISBN 10: 0-7606-0388-X
ISBN 13: 978-0-7606-0388-X

About the Authors

Pam Britton Reese, M.A., CCC-SLP, owns a private practice, CommunicAid Plus, where she provides speech and language services to children and adults. She is also an educational consultant to public and private schools. Pam has over nine years experience in the schools as a speech-language pathologist and teacher of the hearing-impaired. She has worked with children with autism and PDD since 1995. *Autism & PDD: Concept Development* is her fourth publication with LinguiSystems.

Nena C. Challenner, M.Ed., is a Community-Based Instruction Teacher and Inclusion Specialist. She has been a teacher for over 15 years and has taught preschool through second grade. She has worked with children with autism and PDD since 1995. Nena is also a reading consultant at CommunicAid Plus. *Autism & PDD: Concept Development* is her third publication with LinguiSystems.

Dedication

For the children at CommunicAid Plus (CAP Kids!)

Edited by Lauri Whiskeyman
Illustrations by Margaret Warner
Page Layout by Christine Buysse

Table of Contents

Introduction 5

    Shirt 9

    Pants and Shorts 21

    Skirt 33

    Dress 45

    Coat 57

    Shoes 69

    Socks 81

    Hat 93

    Mittens and Gloves 105

    Pajamas and Nightgowns 117

Match-Up Activity 129

Extension Activity 130

Suggested Literature 135

Picture Communication Symbols (PCS) © 1981-2000.
Reprinted with the permission of Mayer-Johnson, Inc., P.O. Box 1579,
Solana Beach, CA 92075-7579, 1-800-588-4548, *www.mayer-johnson.com*

before	page 87
different	page 129
long	pages 25, 38, 50, 88
same	page 129
short	pages 26, 37, 49, 88

Introduction

In our work with children with autism, we were often surprised at misconceptions our students had about the world. For example, when 9-year-old Katie was asked, "What would you do if you saw a house on fire?" she answered, "Roast marshmallows." She had only experienced fire in this way and was unable to perceive that fire might also be dangerous, that it burns, or that it can heat a home. Other children with autism whom we have known didn't recognize a sitting dog as a dog or a rocking chair as a chair. These are concepts that typically-developing children are able to process through observing or listening to information and instantly linking to other learned concepts. We know that children with autism must be taught such language skills as naming attributes, placing words in appropriate categories, and giving descriptions.

It is well documented that children with autism learn more easily when information is presented in a visual format. The picture is constant and the child can view it until the concept is learned, as opposed to the transient nature of speech. Most books published for young children, however, do not teach the concepts the child with autism needs to learn. Although the stories are often engaging and the artwork of museum quality, they too often confuse the child with autism. Foxes that drive? Animals that wear clothing and talk? Cars with eyes? Although amusing, they are not a realistic depiction of our world. Often, too, the art is very complex with many extraneous details. (A list of some books we found that did a good job of teaching concepts is included on page 135.)

Each book in *Autism & PDD: Concept Development* covers 10 concepts around a theme:

- Animals
- Clothing
- Food
- Household Items
- Toys and Entertainment
- Transportation

Specific attributes and features of each concept are illustrated with large pictures, simple sentences, and picture symbols. In addition, there are questions to check comprehension and activities to help the child apply this knowledge to other contexts. These books were developed for professionals who work with children with autism, ages 3 through 8. However, these books can also be used with children who have language delays or language disorders caused by disabilities such as Down syndrome. Parents and caregivers can also use these stories and activities.

How to Use this Book

This book contains concepts about 10 different clothing. Each concept is illustrated in both a large-page and mini-page format for making books to read to the child. We suggest that the large-page format be copied. Place the pages in plastic page protectors. Sliding a thin piece of cardboard or card stock into the pocket between the pages will stiffen the pages and make

Introduction, continued

them easier for young children to turn. Put the pages into folders with brads or three-ring notebooks to create a book. You may want to put a copy of the first page of each unit on the front of the folder or notebook. The mini-pages can be made into small books for the children to take home after they've heard the story at school.

You may want to use all of the concepts in the book at one time to introduce or extend a thematic unit or you can select a specific concept to focus on. For example, a child might know dog and cat, but have no idea what a rabbit is! Remember to go at the child's pace. A child might need many lessons on chairs, for example, before moving on to other concepts in the book.

Comprehension Questions

A variety of comprehension questions (e.g., *yes-no, wh-, how*) follow each concept. The questions can be used in different ways. Some children may only be able to answer the *yes-no* questions. Some children may do better with the *wh-* and *how* questions. You can ask the questions after each concept is taught or after each page. If a child has difficulty answering a question, go through the targeted concept again and help him or her find the answer. Cue the child by pointing to the picture and/or text as you ask the question again.

Generalization Pages

Each concept has a generalization exercise. This exercise is designed to check the child's comprehension of the concept as well as to extend understanding of the concept to different forms and views. Many of the children we work with understand only one form of a concept: "That is a cat. That cat is gray. Thus, all cats must be gray or they are not cats." As you can see, that is a false generalization. By presenting variations of the same concept such as size, color, and position, the child learns to expand his or her mental definition of the concept.

After you read about the targeted concept, make a copy of the generalization page for the child. Read the directions aloud and have the child complete the page. Then encourage the child to describe the circled concepts. Depending on the child's level, the responses could be as simple as labeling "shirt" or as elaborate as "The shirt has long sleeves." You can also use the pictures on this page to point out the differences between the circled concepts.

Extension Activity

This activity is designed to extend instruction for any of the concepts in the book. Directions are found on the activity pages.

Introduction, continued

Suggested Literature

We have included a list of children's literature to help extend and promote generalization of the concepts to other contexts. These books were carefully chosen because of their simple text and realistic pictures. It is important to provide as many opportunities as possible for the child with autism to see and hear the concept. We have found that repeated exposure to the concepts in *Autism & PDD: Concept Development*, followed by other books with different pictures and texts, aids the child with autism in generalizing the concept to different contexts.

Closing

Remember that the concepts covered in the book can be taught in classrooms as well as group or individual therapy sessions. We hope that the children you work with enjoy the books as much as our students and clients do.

Pam and Nena

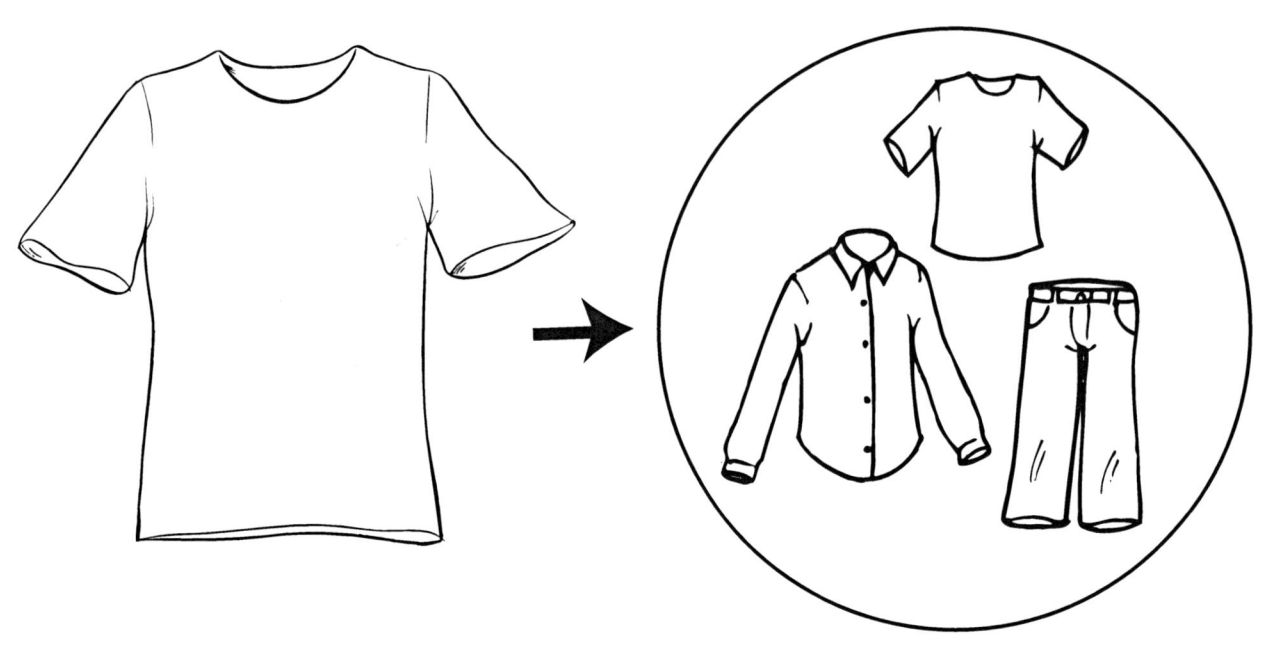

A shirt is clothing.

People wear shirts.

 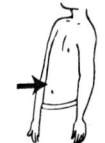 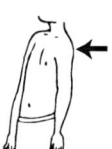 

A shirt covers the front, back, and arms.

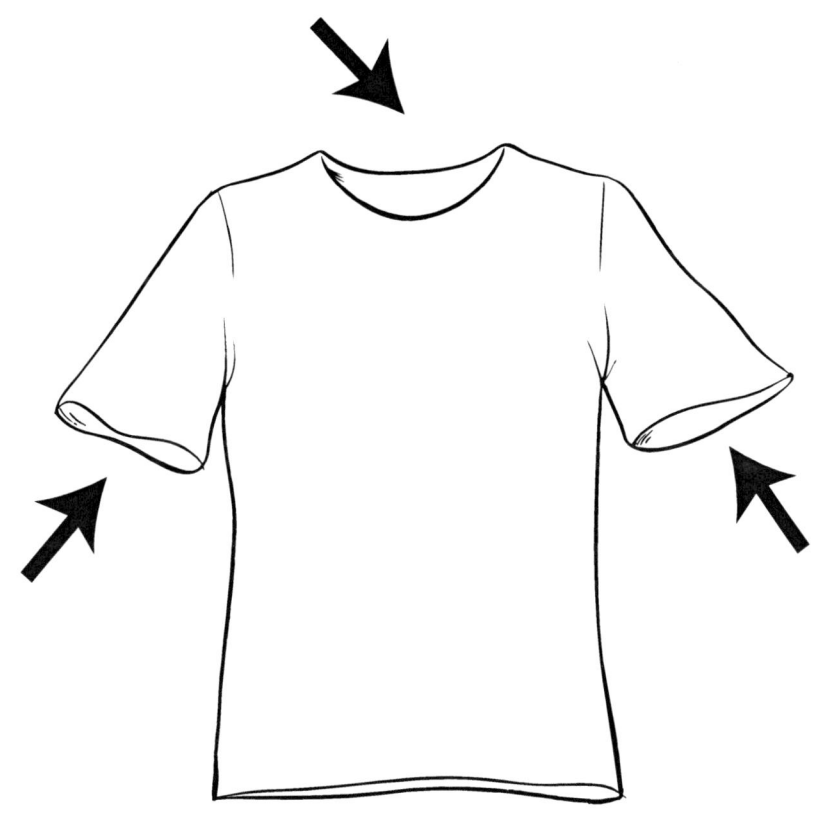

A shirt has holes for the head and arms.

Some shirts have buttons and collars.

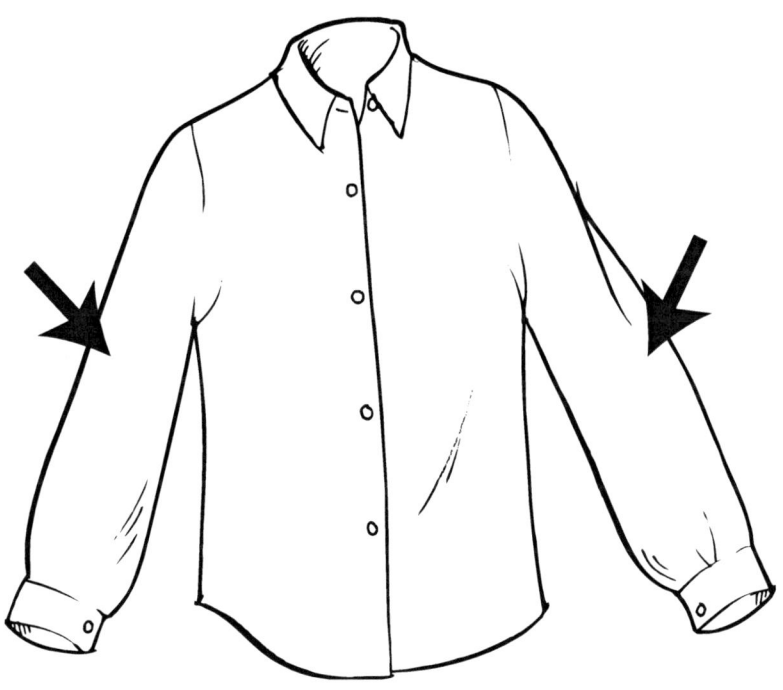

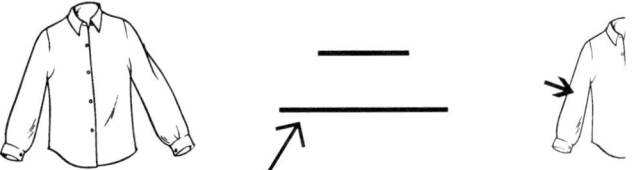

Some shirts have long sleeves.

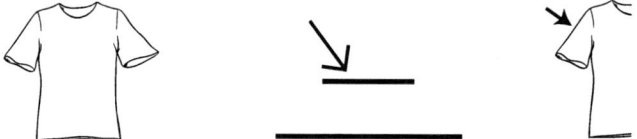

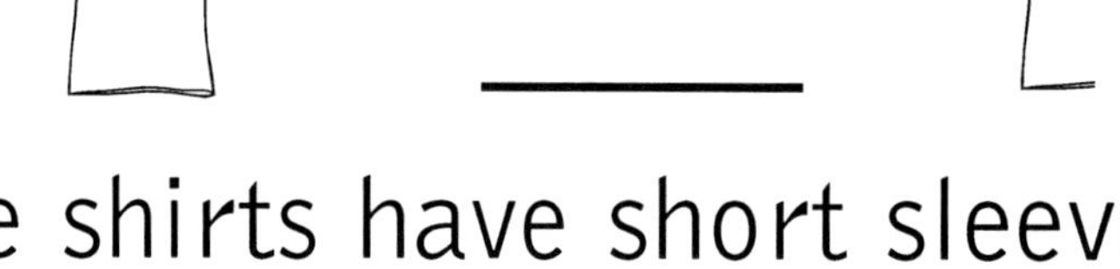

Some shirts have short sleeves.

Shirt

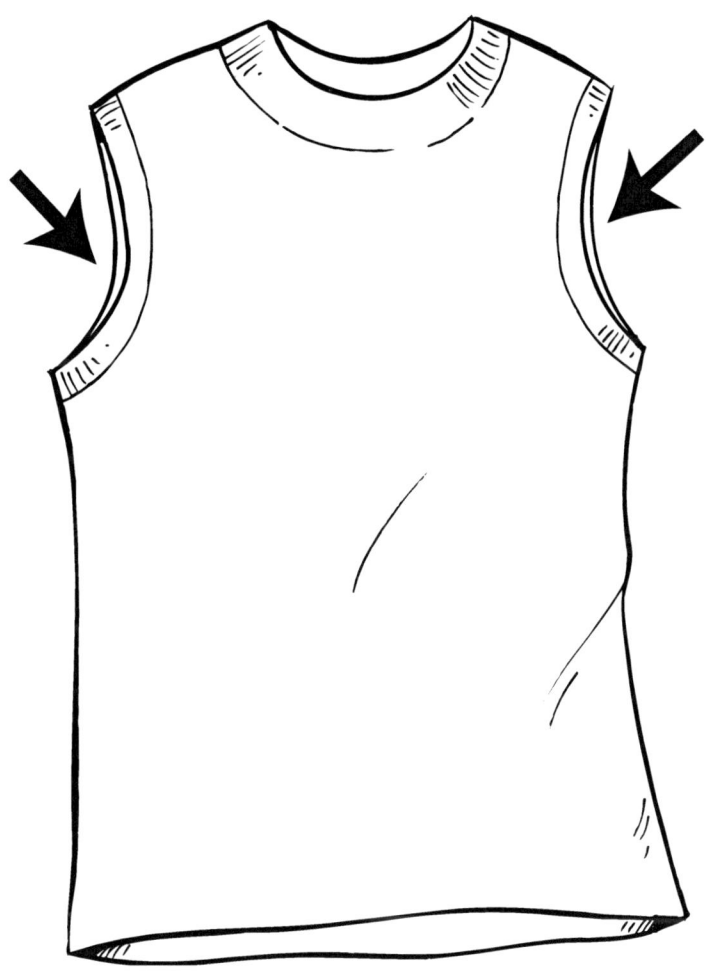

Some shirts have no sleeves.

Concept: Shirt

Yes-No Questions

1. Do people wear shirts?
2. Does a shirt have holes for the head and arms?
3. Do all shirts have sleeves?
4. Does a shirt cover your legs?
5. Is a shirt clothing?
6. Do some shirts have buttons?
7. Is a shirt a toy?
8. Do some shirts have collars?
9. Does a shirt have holes for legs?
10. Do only girls wear shirts?

Wh- and How Questions

1. Who wears a shirt?
2. Why does a shirt have holes?
3. What does a shirt cover?
4. Which sleeve covers your whole arm?
5. What is a shirt?

Shirt Generalization Page

Circle the shirts. Put an X on each picture that is not a shirt.

Shirt
Concept Development

Shirt Mini-Book

Copy this page. Cut apart the boxes on the dotted lines. Put the story in order to make a little book and staple.

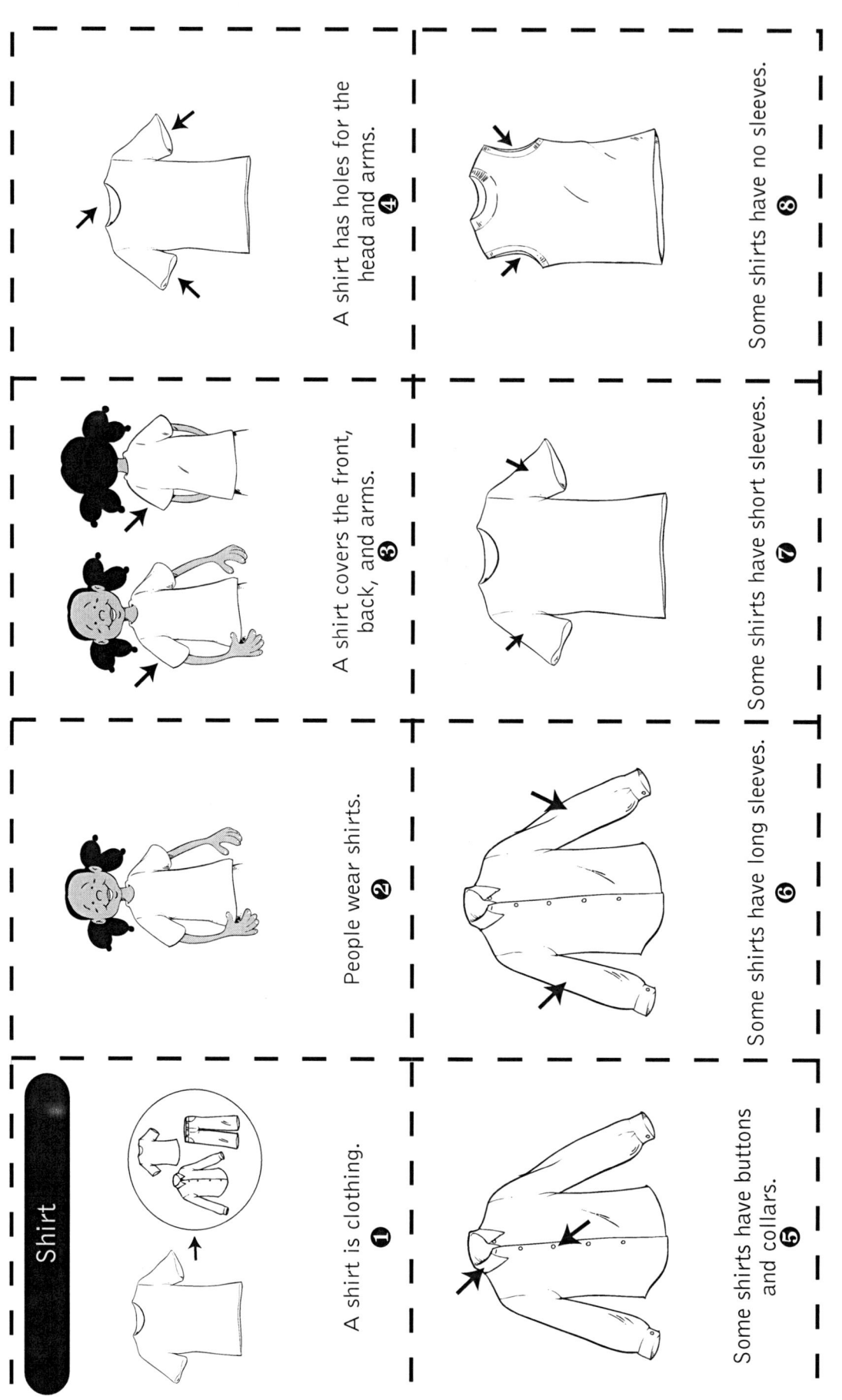

Pants and Shorts

Pants and shorts are clothing.

People wear pants and shorts.

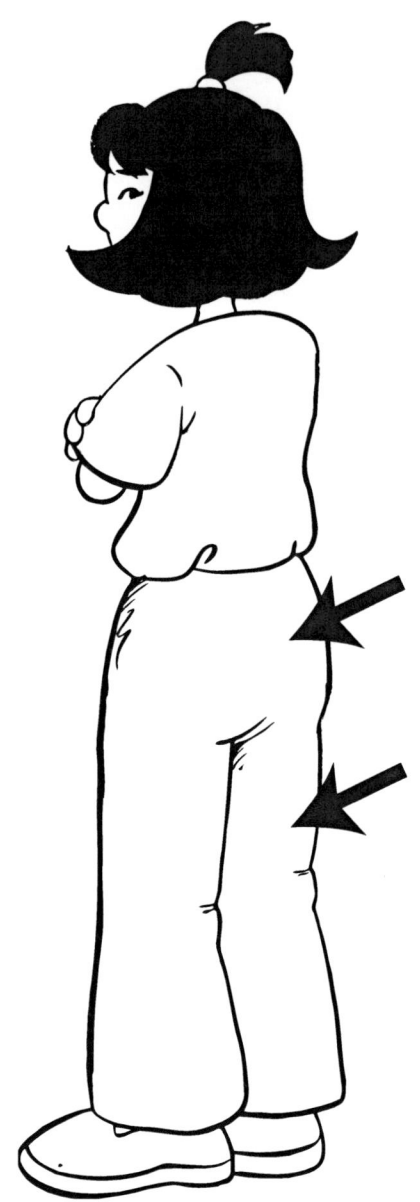

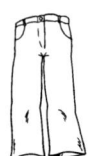   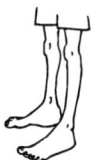

Pants and shorts cover bottoms and legs.

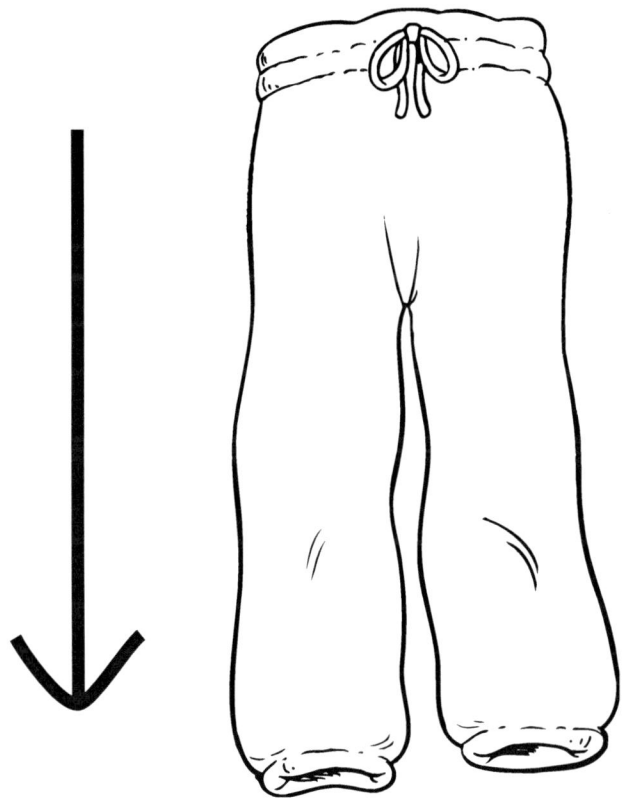

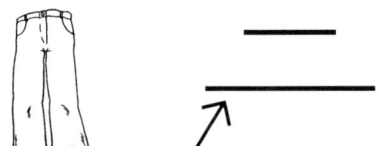

Pants are long.

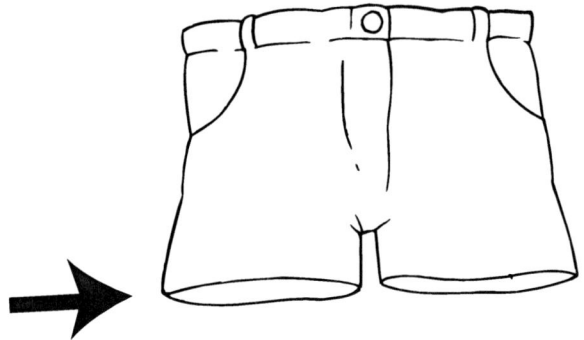

 Shorts are short.

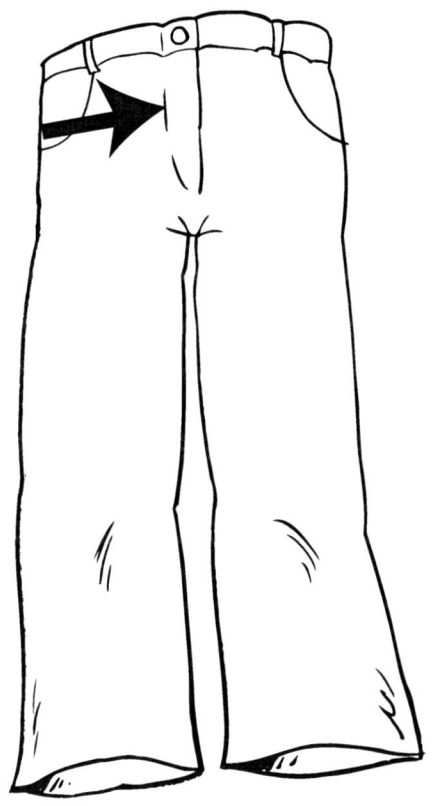
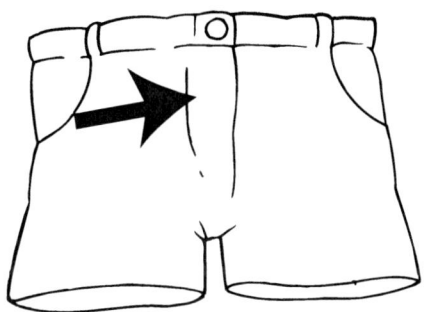

  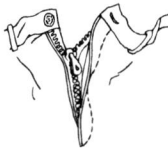

Some pants and shorts have zippers.

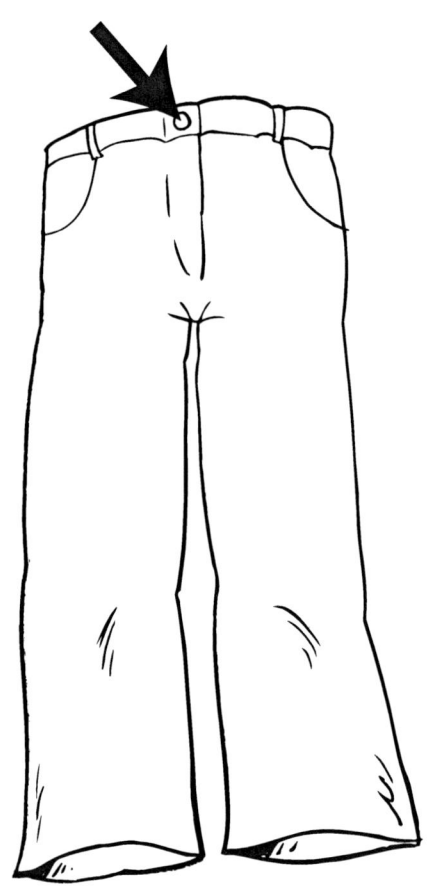

Some pants and shorts have buttons or snaps.

Boys and girls wear pants and shorts.

Concept: Pants and Shorts

Yes-No Questions

1. Are pants clothing?
2. Are shorts long?
3. Are pants long?
4. Do animals wear pants and shorts?
5. Can a girl wear pants?
6. Can a boy wear shorts?
7. Do all pants and shorts have zippers?
8. Do pants cover your legs?
9. Do pants and shorts have sleeves?
10. Are pants and shorts food?

Wh- and How Questions

1. Who wears pants and shorts?
2. When do people wear shorts?
3. What do pants and shorts cover?
4. How are pants and shorts different?
5. What do people do with pants and shorts?

Pants and Shorts Generalization Page

Circle the pants and shorts. Put an X on each picture that is not pants or shorts.

Pants and Shorts
Concept Development

Pants and Shorts Mini-Book

Copy this page. Cut apart the boxes on the dotted lines. Put the story in order to make a little book and staple.

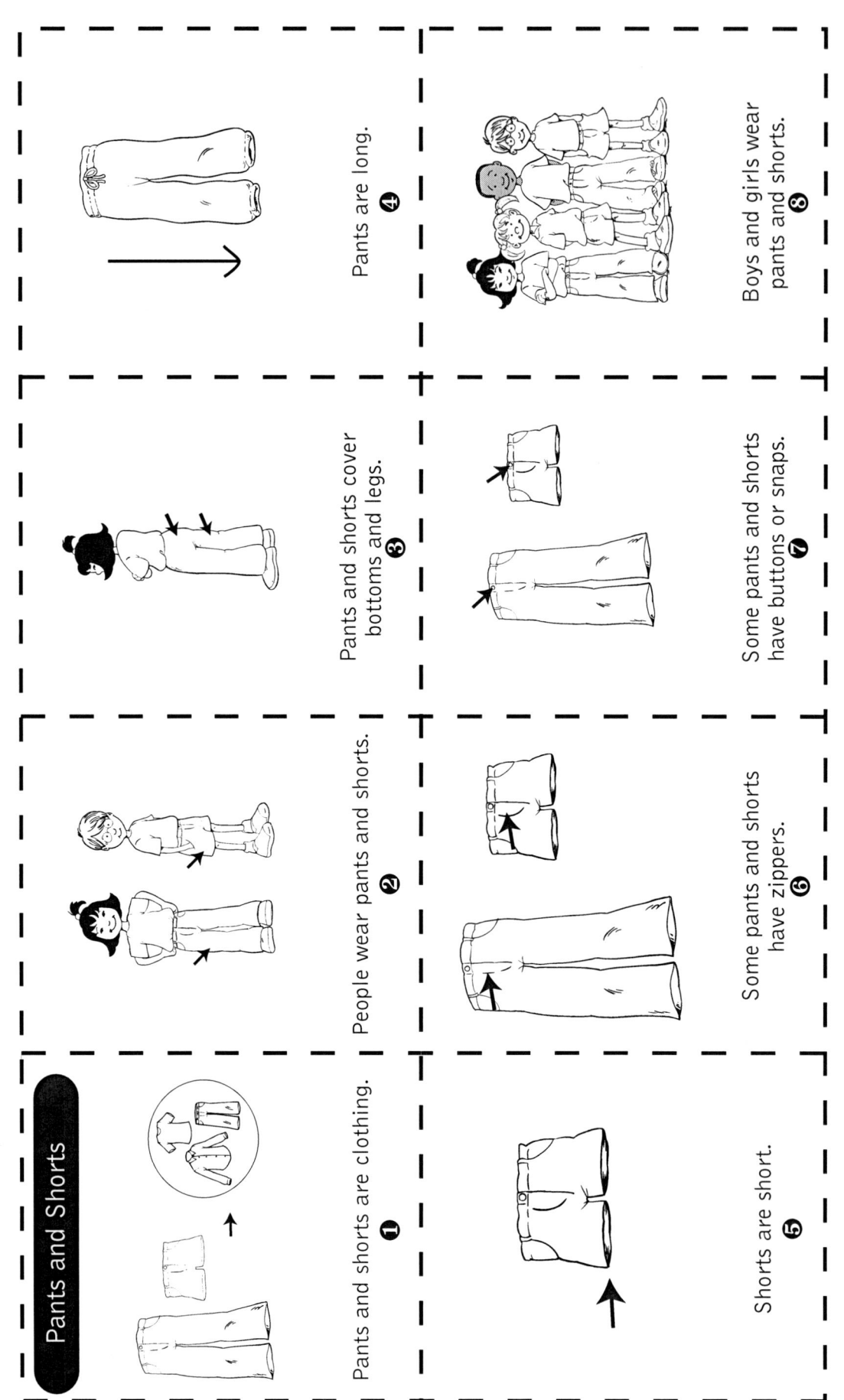

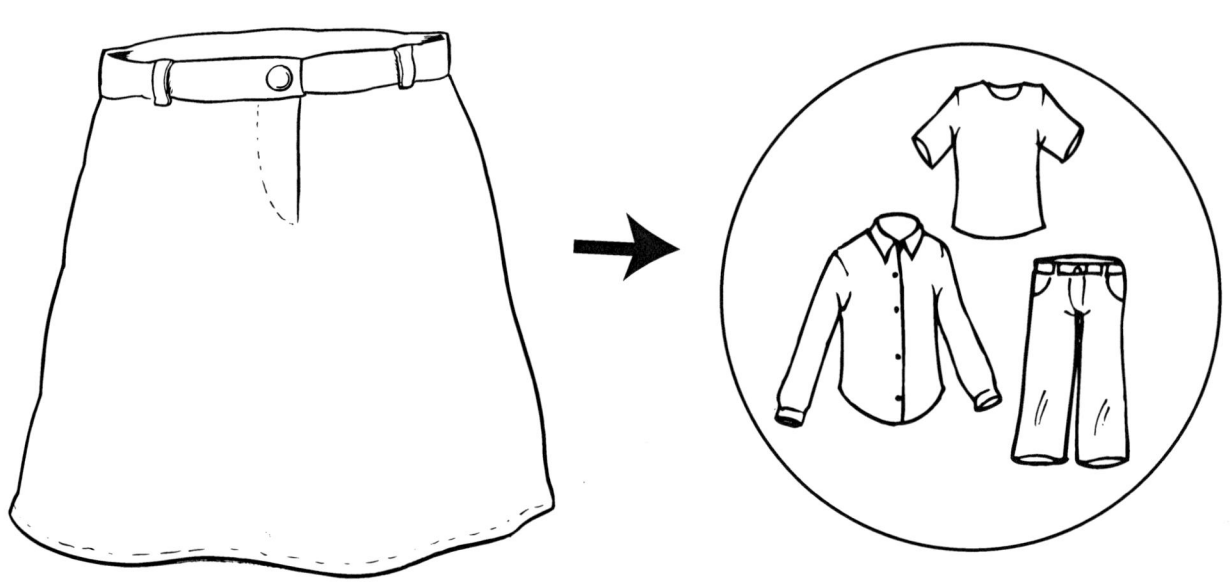

A skirt is clothing.

Women and girls wear skirts.

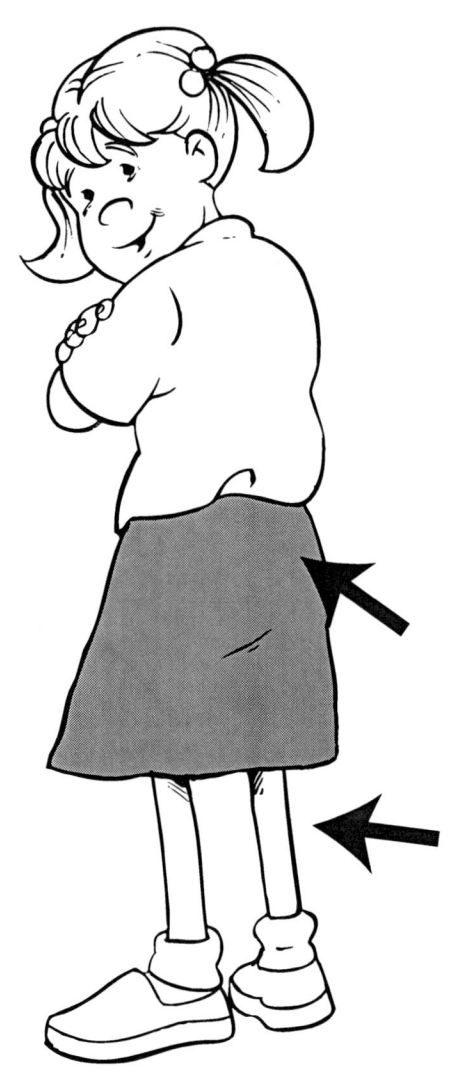

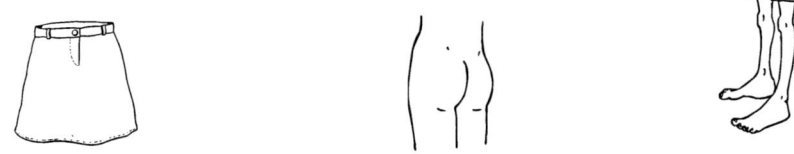

Skirts cover bottoms and legs.

Skirt

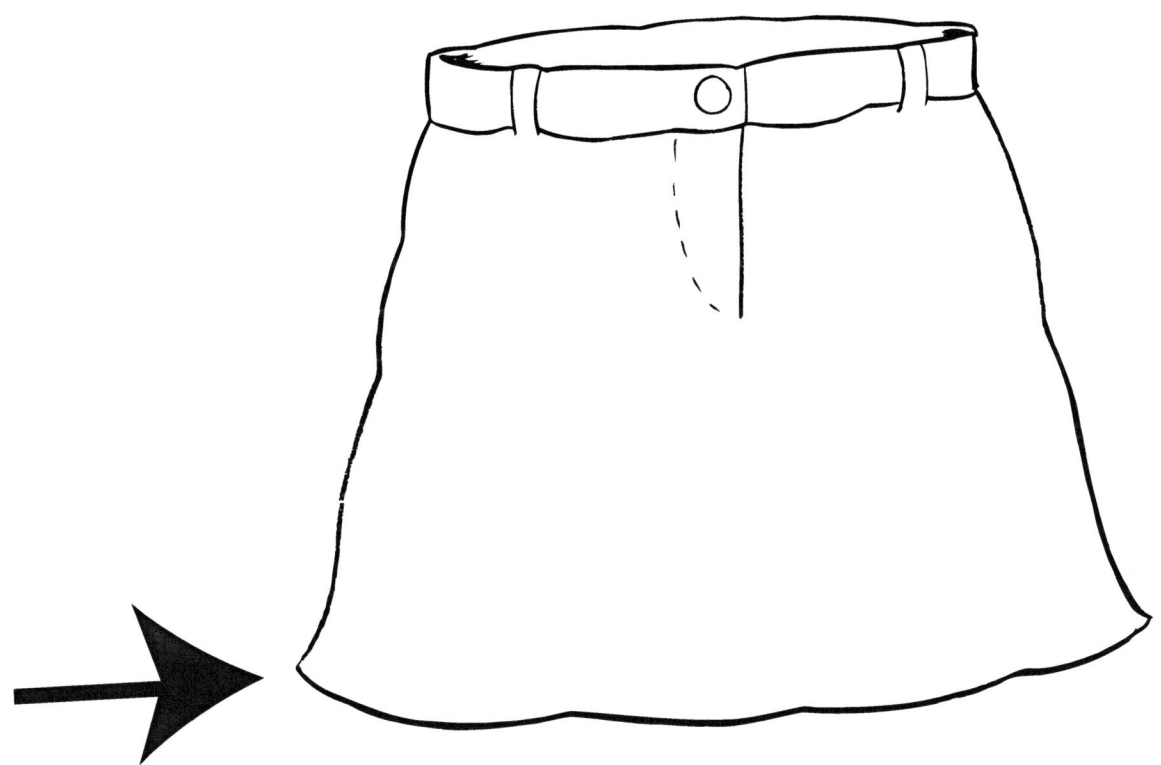

Some skirts are short.

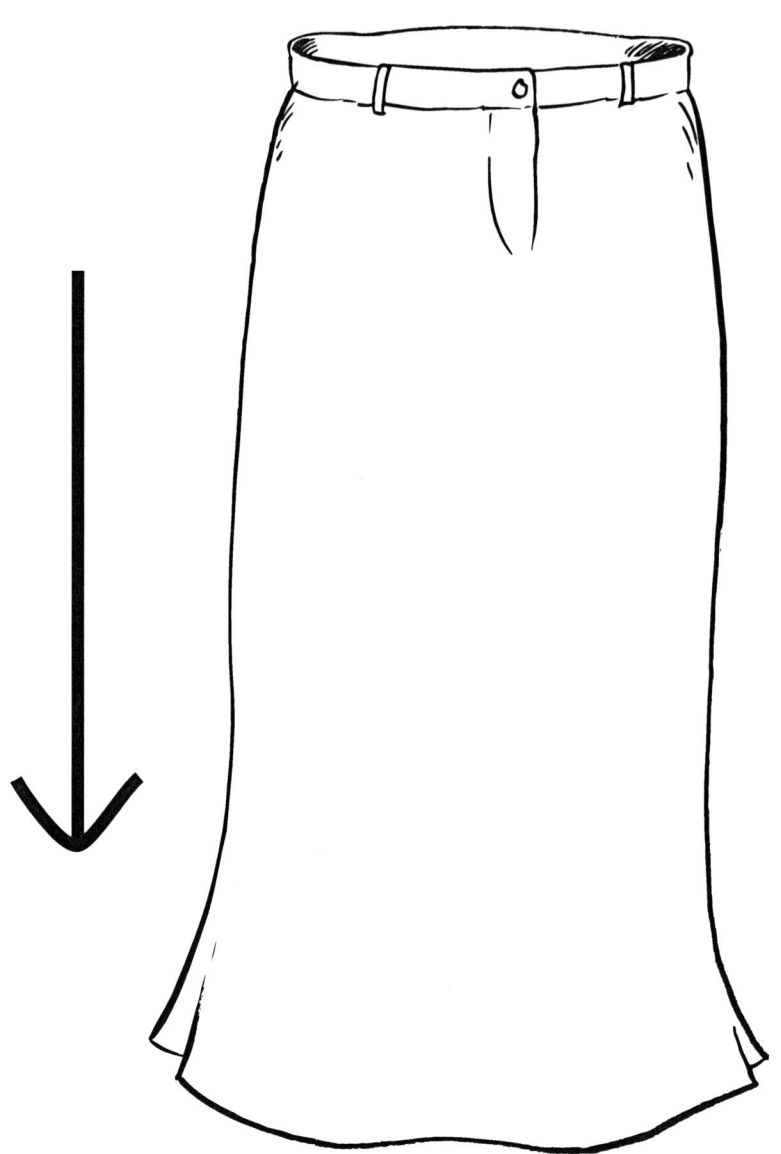

Some skirts are long.

Some skirts have buttons and a zipper.

All of these are skirts.

You need to wear a shirt with a skirt.

Concept: Skirt

Yes-No Questions

1. Do girls wear skirts?
2. Do boys wear skirts?
3. Is a skirt clothing?
4. Are all skirts long?
5. Do skirts cover your arms?
6. Do women wear skirts?
7. Can a skirt have buttons?
8. Can a skirt have sleeves?
9. Can a skirt be short?
10. Does a skirt cover your neck?

Wh- and How Questions

1. What do you need to wear with a skirt?
2. What does a skirt cover?
3. Who wears a skirt?
4. What other clothing covers bottoms and legs?
5. What clothing can be short or long?

Skirt Generalization Page

Circle the skirts. Put an X on each picture that is not a skirt.

Skirt Mini-Book

Copy this page. Cut apart the boxes on the dotted lines. Put the story in order to make a little book and staple.

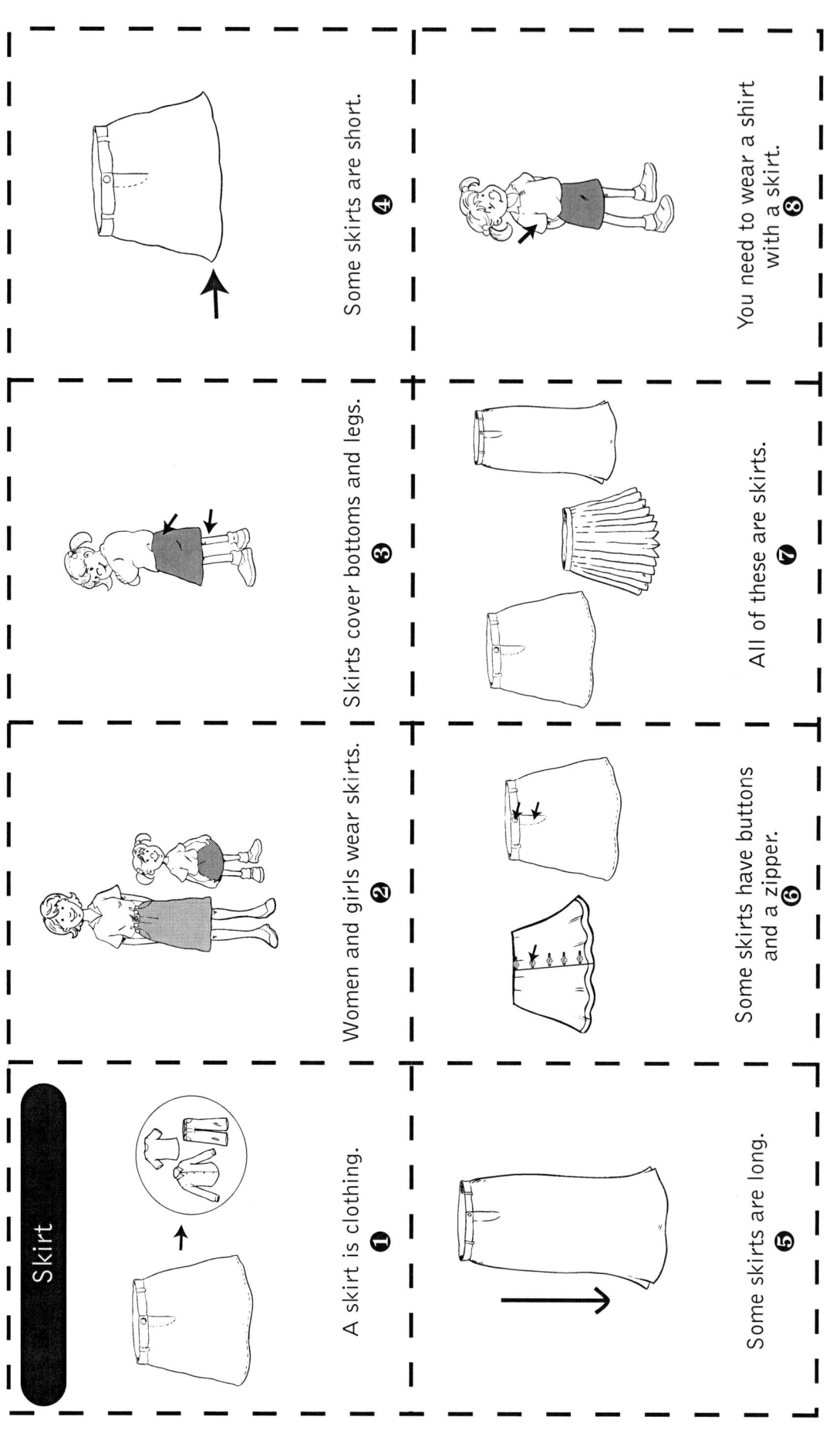

1. A skirt is clothing.
2. Women and girls wear skirts.
3. Skirts cover bottoms and legs.
4. Some skirts are short.
5. Some skirts are long.
6. Some skirts have buttons and a zipper.
7. All of these are skirts.
8. You need to wear a shirt with a skirt.

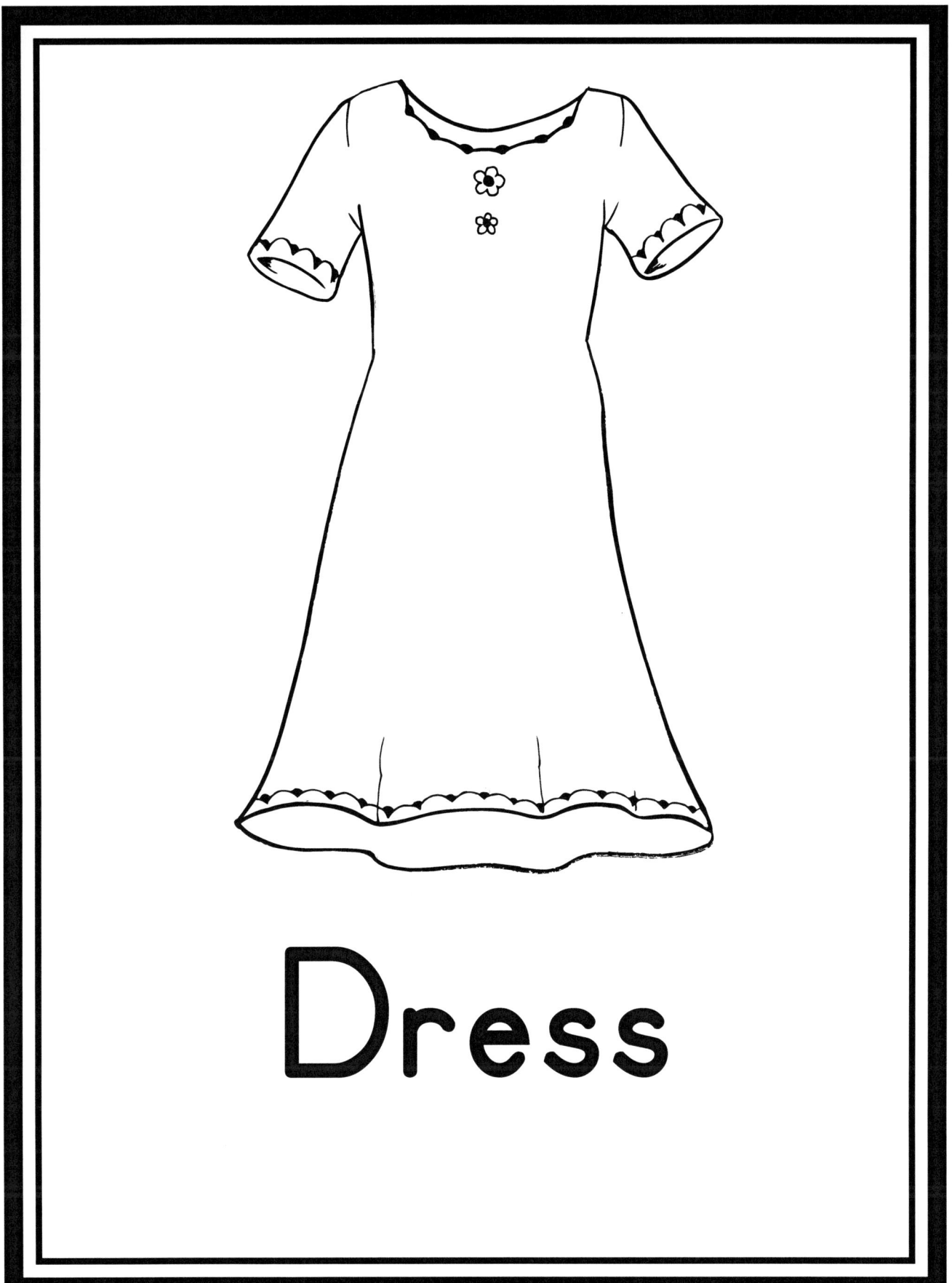

A dress is clothing.

Women and girls wear dresses.

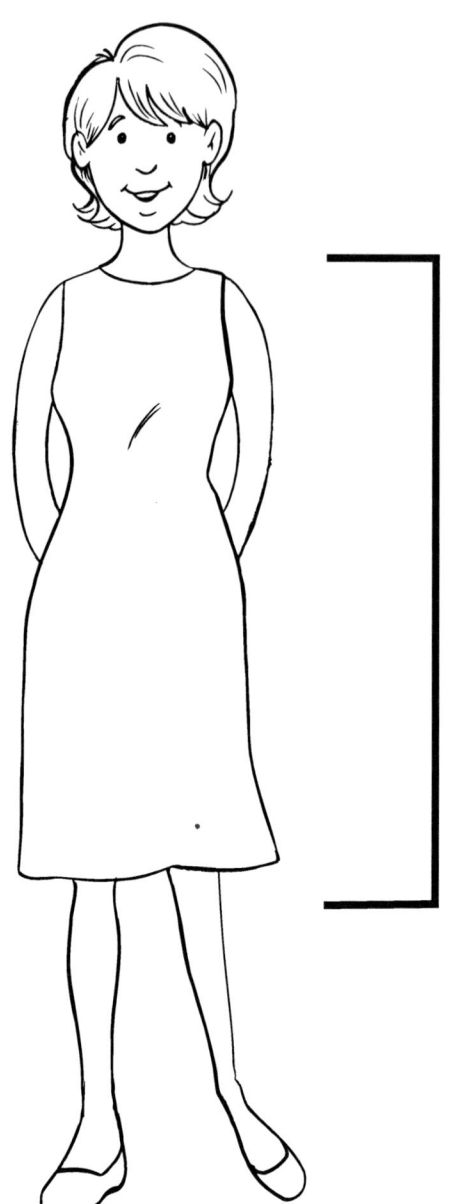

Dresses cover your body.

Dress
Concept Development

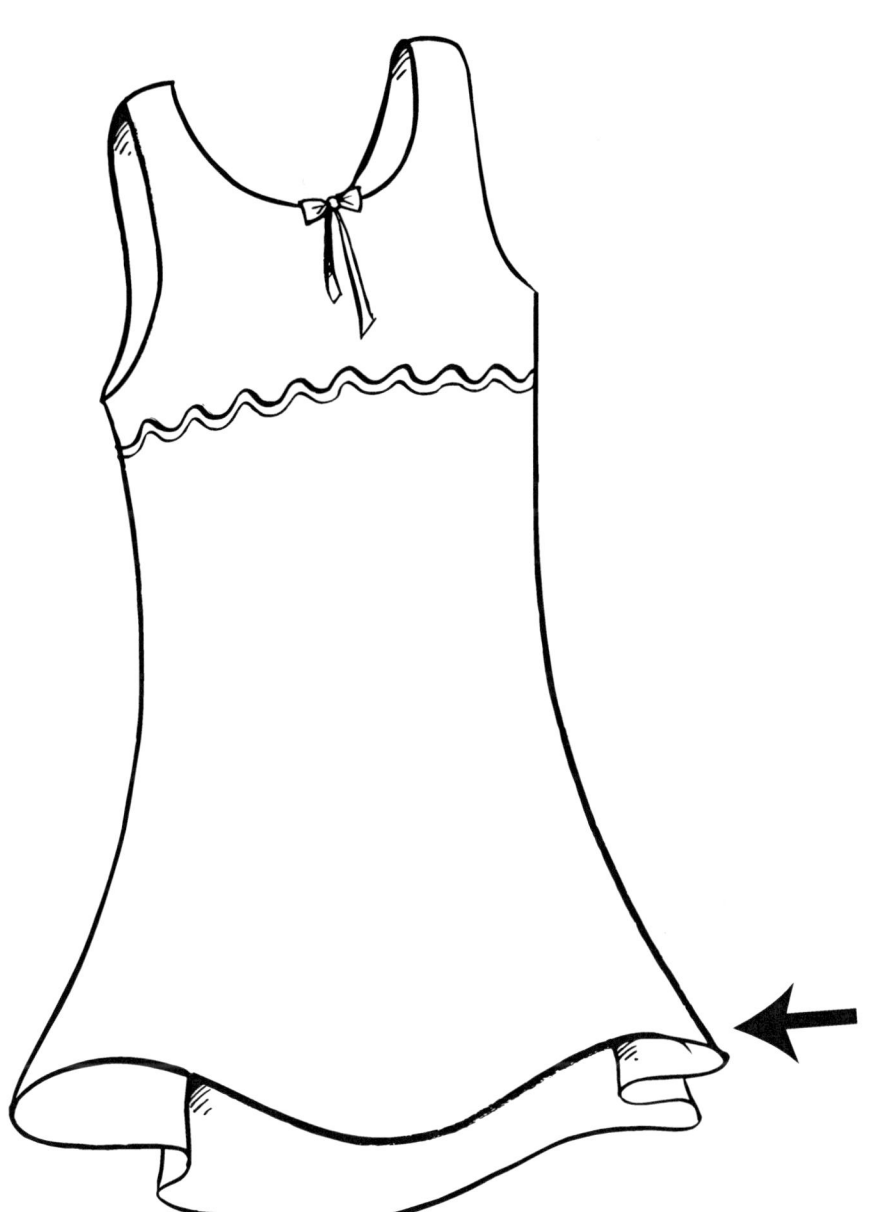

Some dresses are short.

Some dresses are long.

 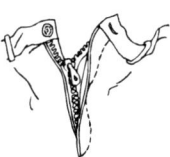

Some dresses have buttons and a zipper.

Some dresses have sleeves.

All of these are dresses.

Concept: Dress

Yes-No Questions

1. Do boys wear dresses?
2. Do girls wear dresses?
3. Do women wear dresses?
4. Are dresses toys?
5. Do dresses cover your hair?
6. Do dresses cover your body?
7. Are some dresses long?
8. Are some dresses short?
9. Do all dresses have sleeves?
10. Do dresses have holes for arms?

Wh- and How Questions

1. Who wears a dress?
2. What do dresses cover?
3. What is a dress?
4. What clothing do women and girls wear?
5. Why do some dresses have buttons and zippers?

Dress Generalization Page

Circle the dresses. Put an X on each picture that is not a dress.

Dress
Concept Development

Dress Mini-Book

Copy this page. Cut apart the boxes on the dotted lines. Put the story in order to make a little book and staple.

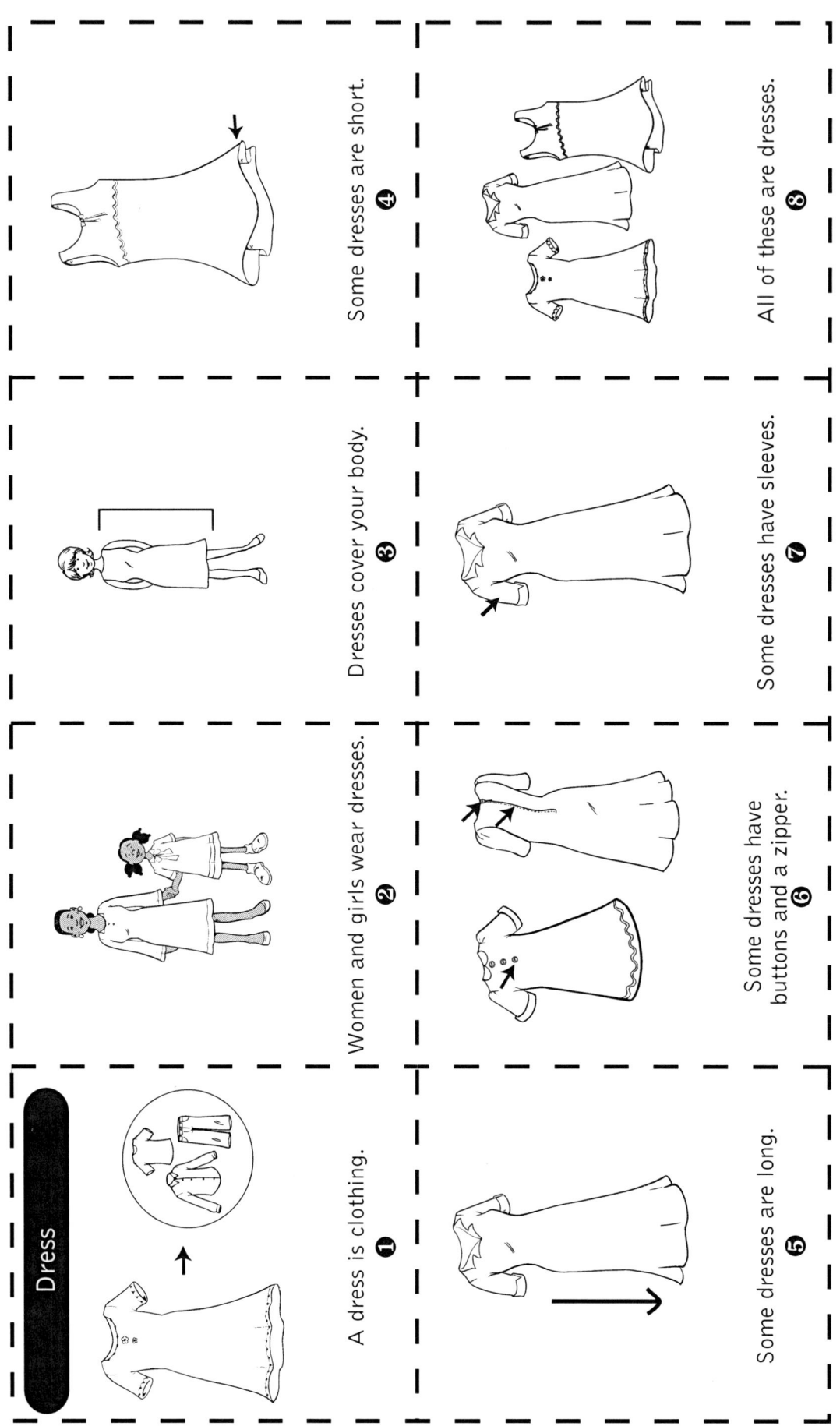

Dress
Concept Development

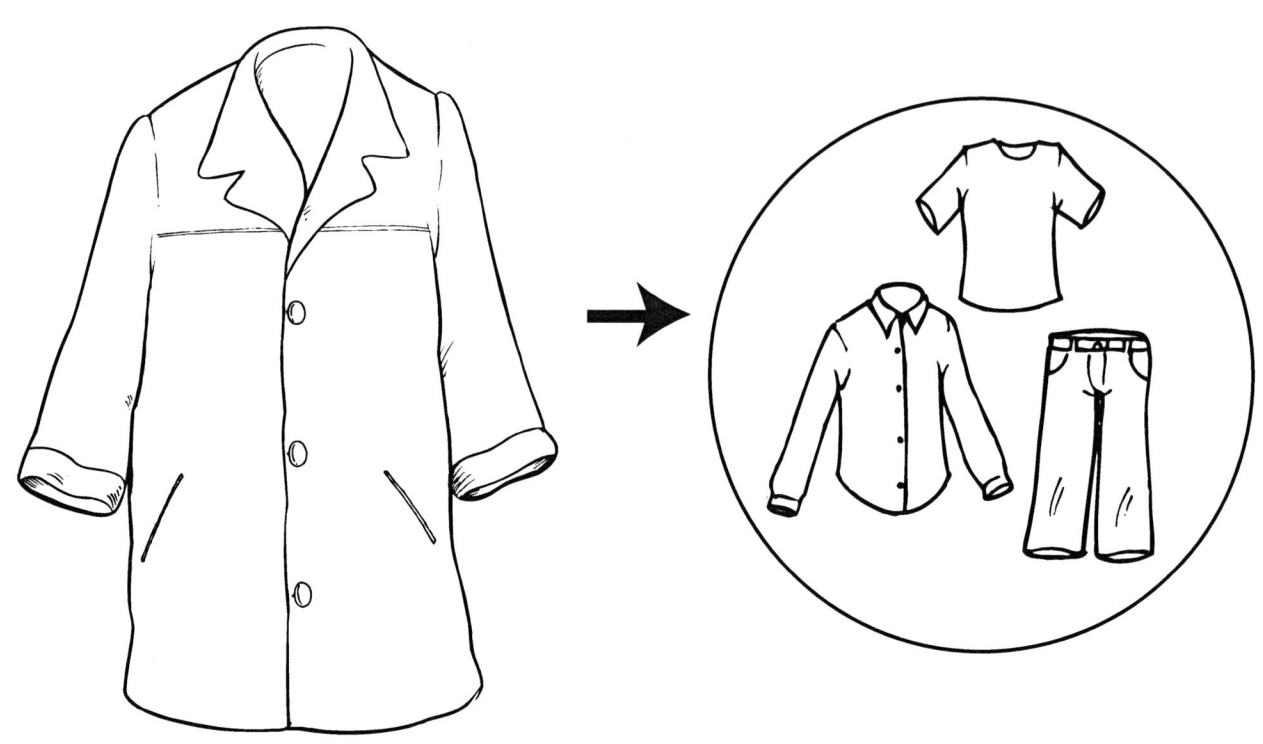

A coat is clothing.

People wear coats.

Coat

Coats go over clothes.

People wear coats when it is cold.

Coats keep people warm.

People wear coats outside.

Coat

Some coats have buttons or a zipper.

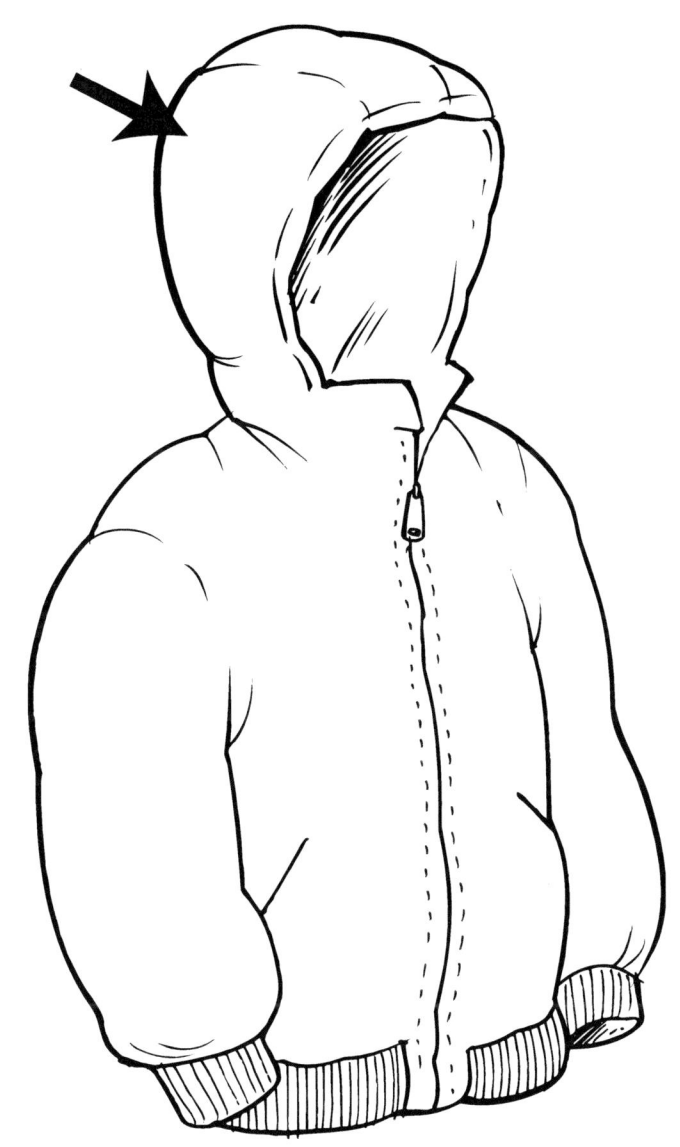

Sometimes coats have hoods.

Concept: Coat

Yes-No Questions

1. Do coats go under clothes?
2. Are coats clothing?
3. Do animals wear coats?
4. Do people wear coats inside?
5. Do people wear coats outside?
6. Can a coat have a hood?
7. Do all coats have zippers?
8. Do some coats have zippers?
9. Do coats keep people cold?
10. Do coats keep people warm?

Wh- and How Questions

1. Who wears a coat?
2. Why do people wear coats?
3. Where do people wear coats?
4. What clothing goes over clothes?
5. When do people wear coats?

Coat Generalization Page

Circle the coats. Put an X on each picture that is not a coat.

Coat Mini-Book

Copy this page. Cut apart the boxes on the dotted lines. Put the story in order to make a little book and staple.

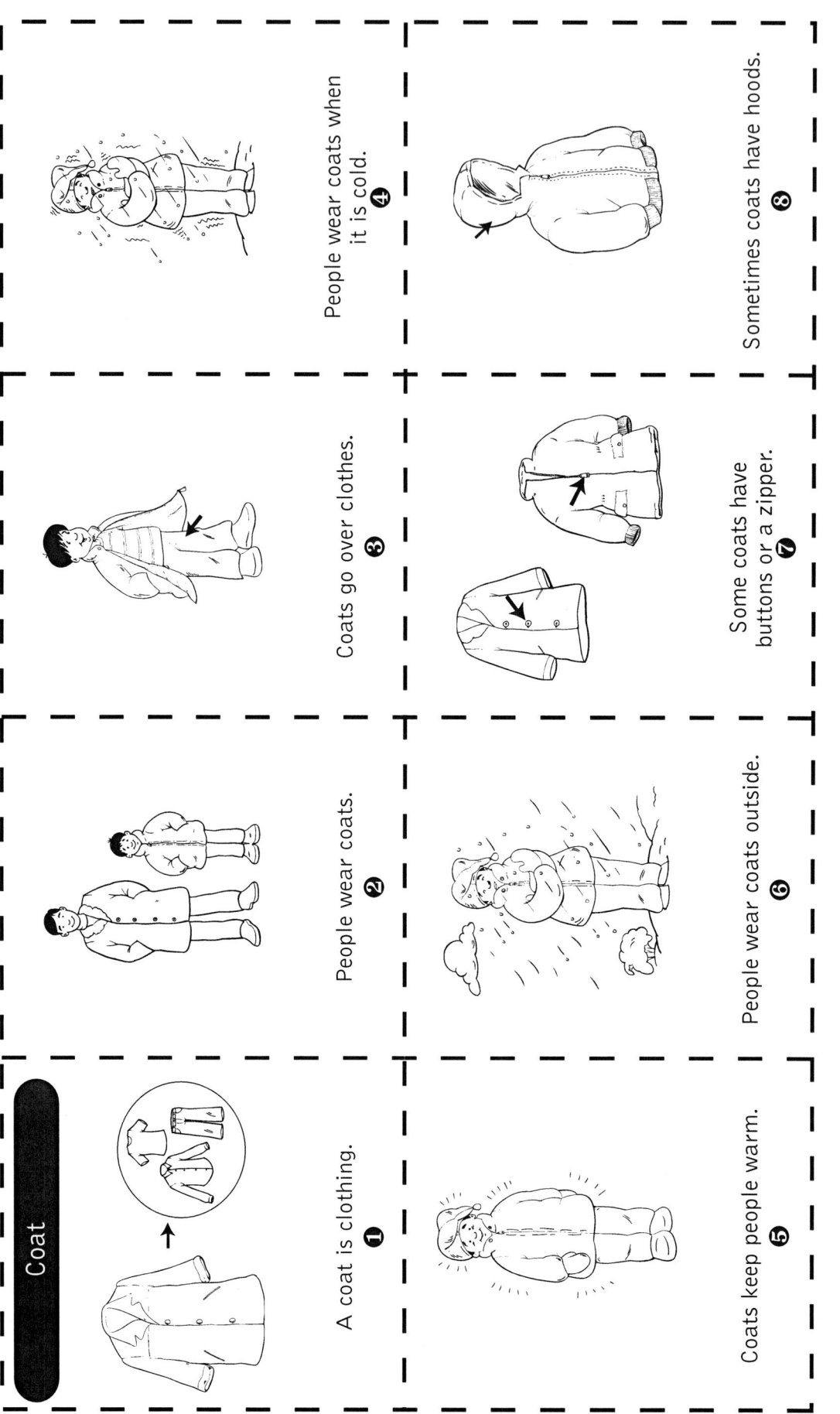

1. A coat is clothing.
2. People wear coats.
3. Coats go over clothes.
4. People wear coats when it is cold.
5. Coats keep people warm.
6. People wear coats outside.
7. Some coats have buttons or a zipper.
8. Sometimes coats have hoods.

Shoes

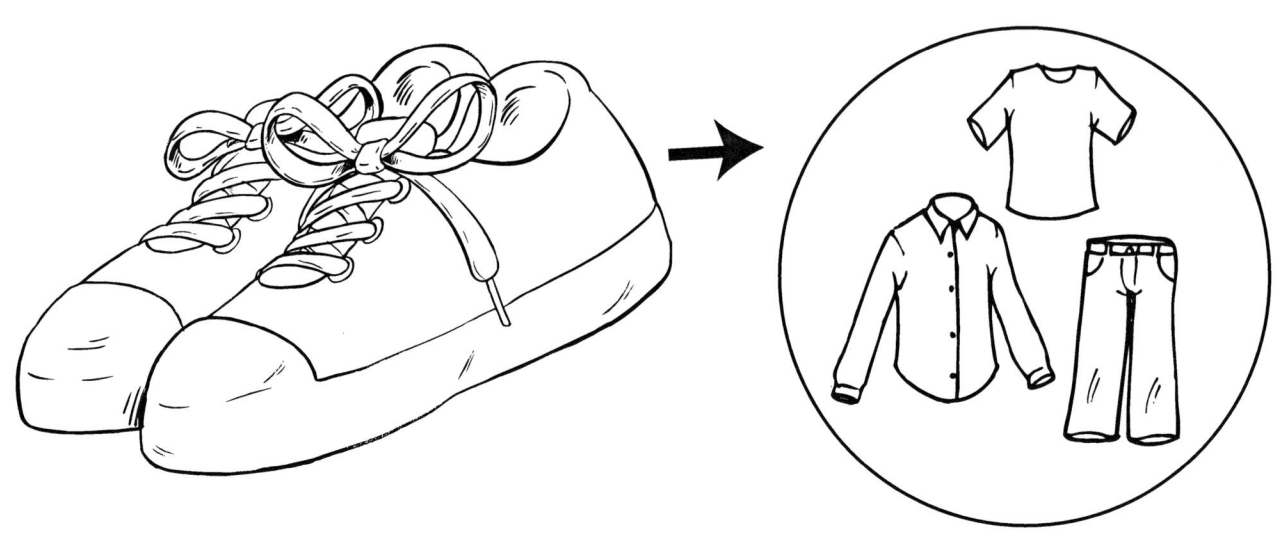

Shoes are clothing.

People wear shoes.

Shoes cover feet.

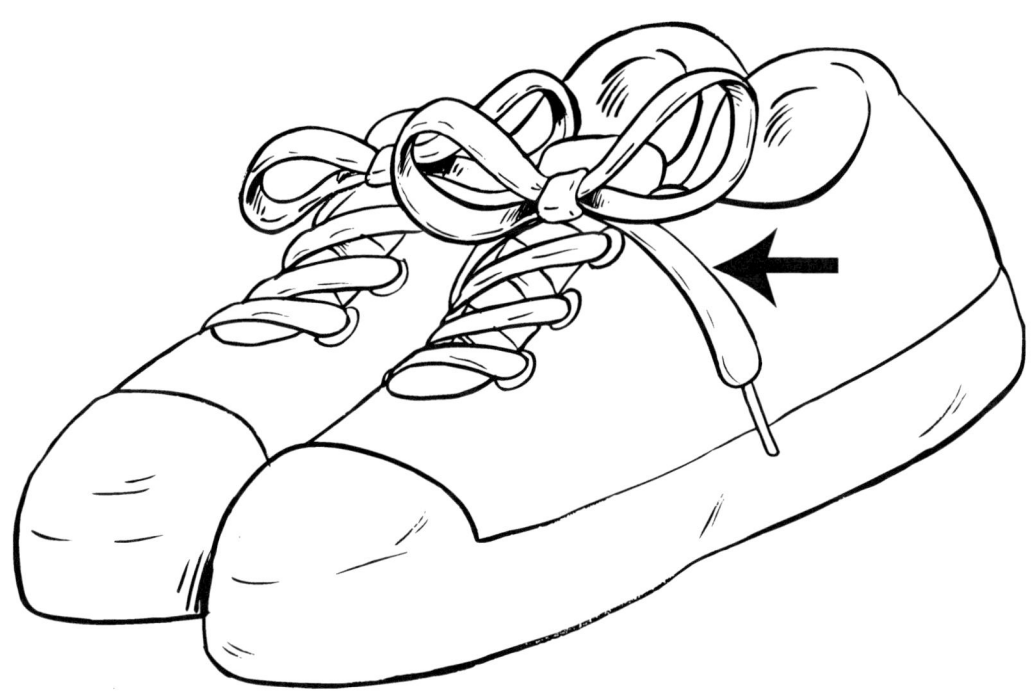

Some shoes have laces to tie.

Some shoes have buckles.

All of these are shoes.

People wear socks with shoes.

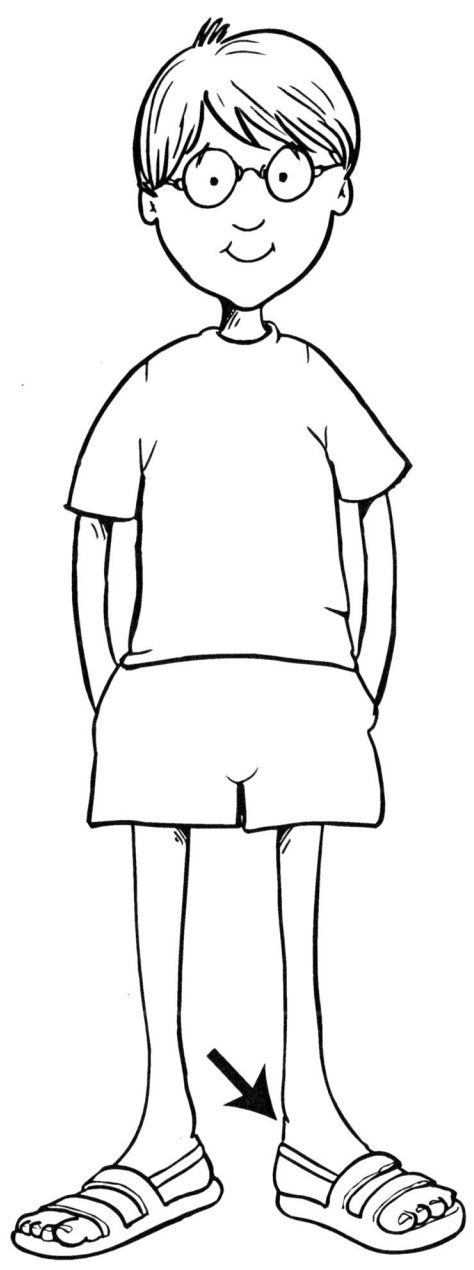

You don't need socks with sandals!

Concept: Shoes

Yes-No Questions

1. Do shoes cover hands?
2. Are shoes clothing?
3. Do people wear shoes?
4. Do you need socks with sandals?
5. Do shoes cover feet?
6. Are buckles on some shoes?
7. Do animals wear shoes?
8. Do people wear socks with shoes?
9. Do all shoes look the same?
10. Do all shoes have laces?

Wh- and How Questions

1. Who wears shoes?
2. What do shoes cover?
3. Which shoes do not need socks?
4. Why do people wear shoes?
5. How many shoes do you wear?

Shoes Generalization Page

Circle the shoes. Put an X on each picture that is not shoes.

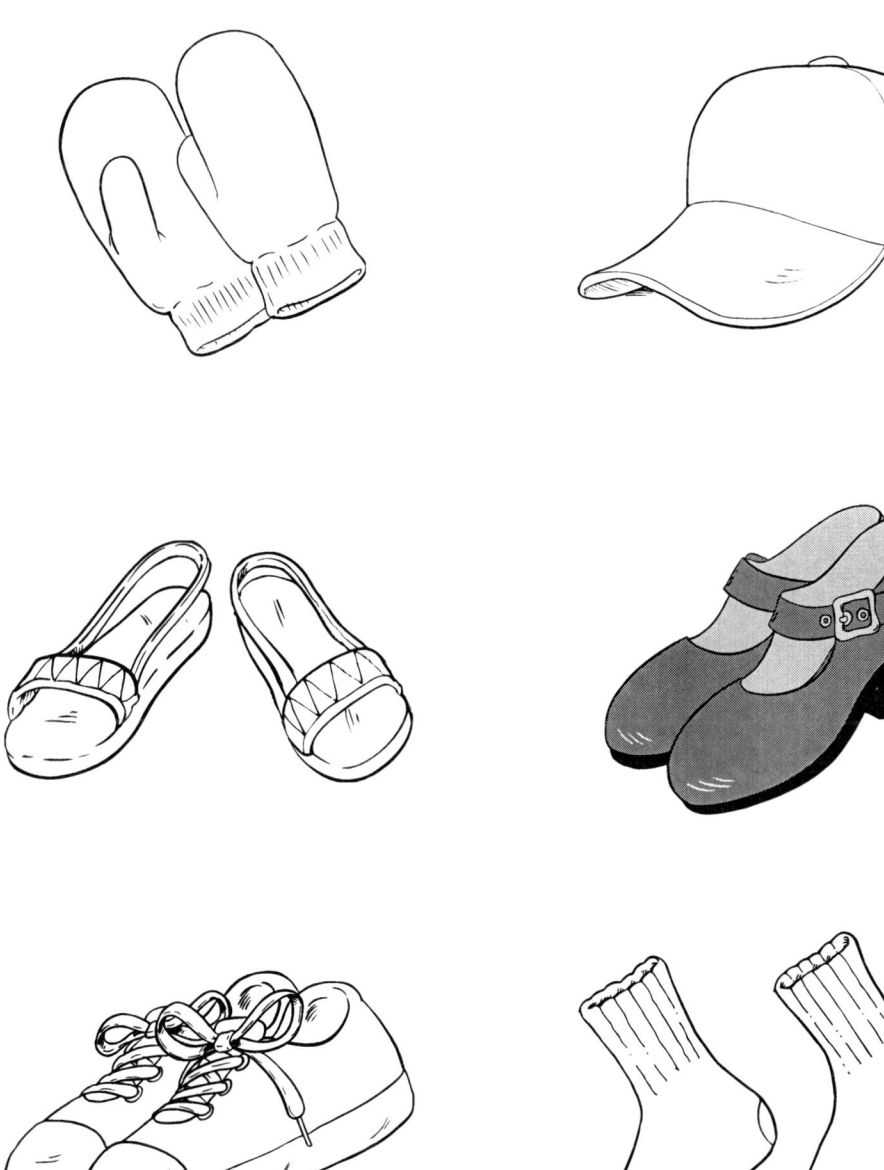

Shoes
Concept Development

Shoes Mini-Book

Copy this page. Cut apart the boxes on the dotted lines. Put the story in order to make a little book and staple.

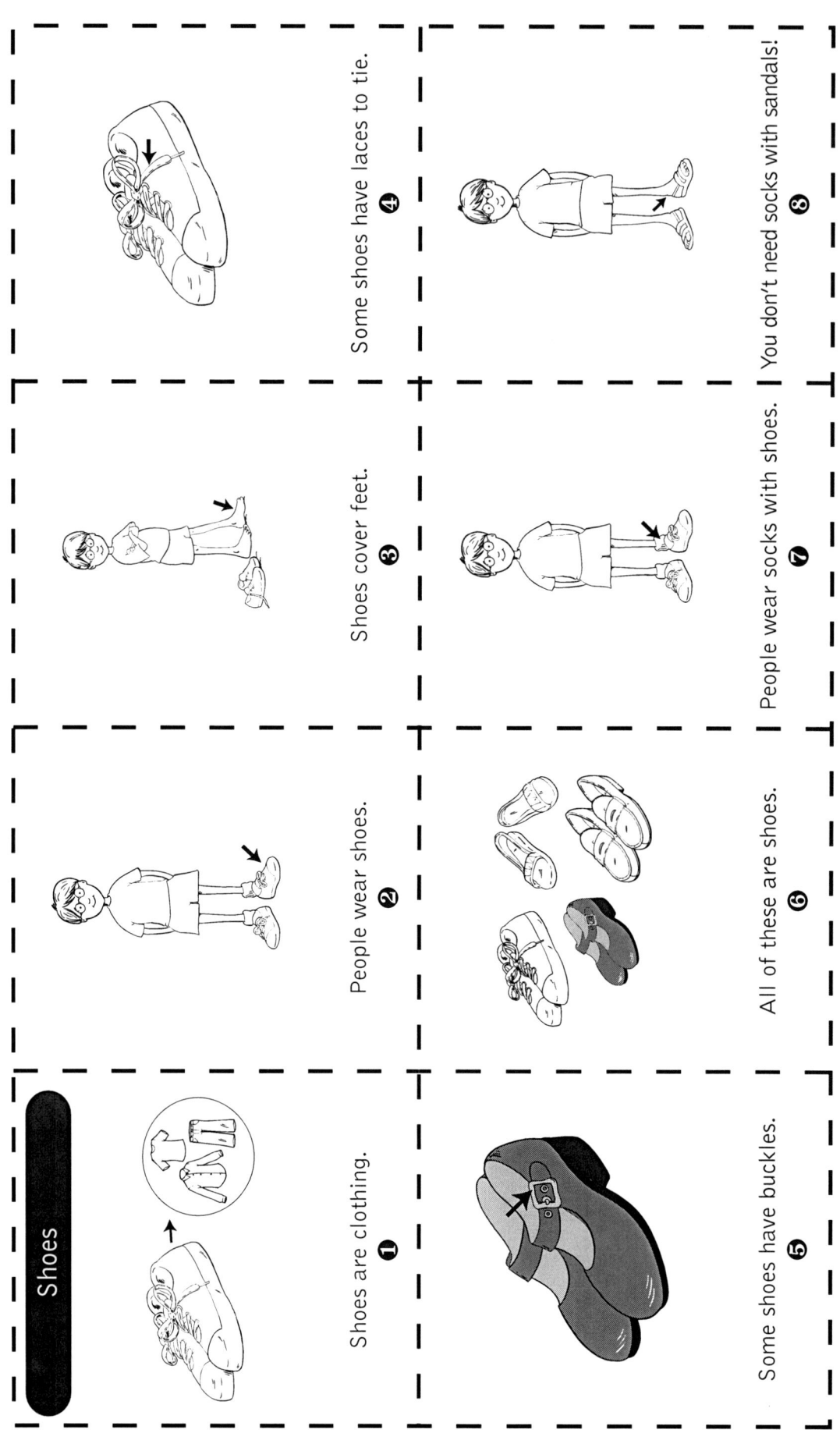

Socks

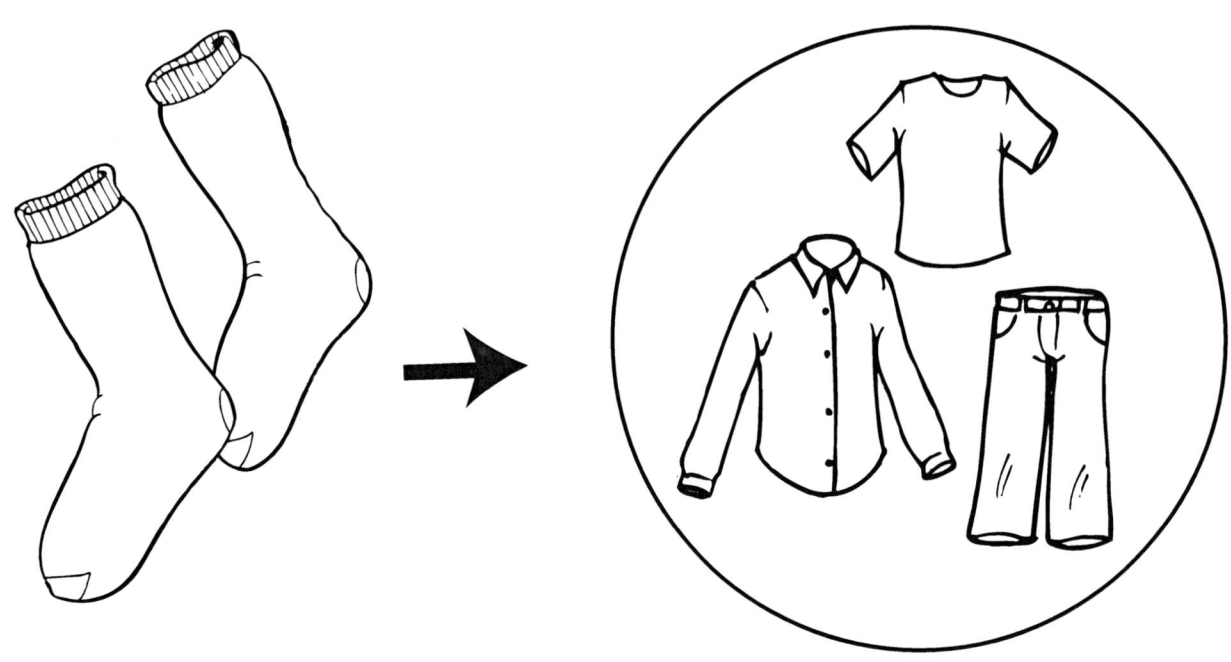

Socks are clothing.

People wear socks.

pair

2

Two socks are a pair.

Socks cover feet.

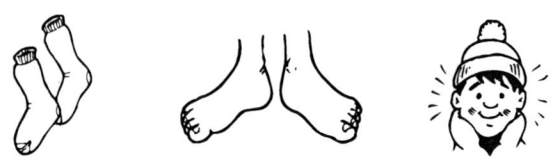

Socks keep feet warm.

  •

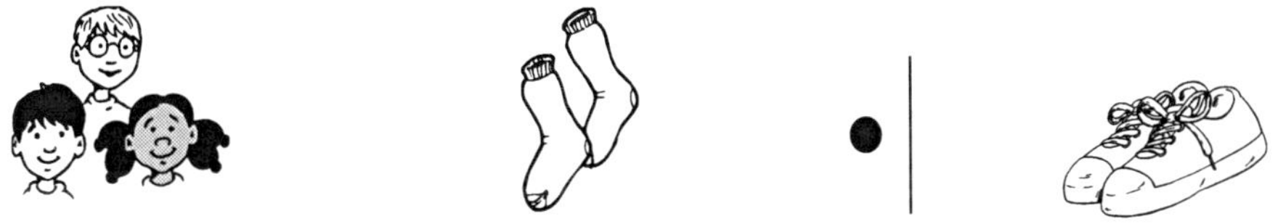

People put on socks before shoes.

Socks

 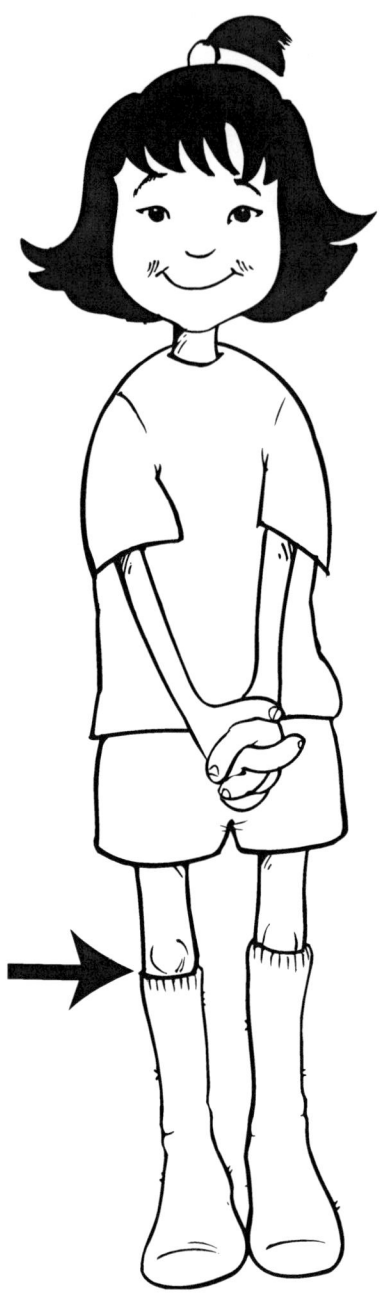

 Some socks are short.  Some socks are long.

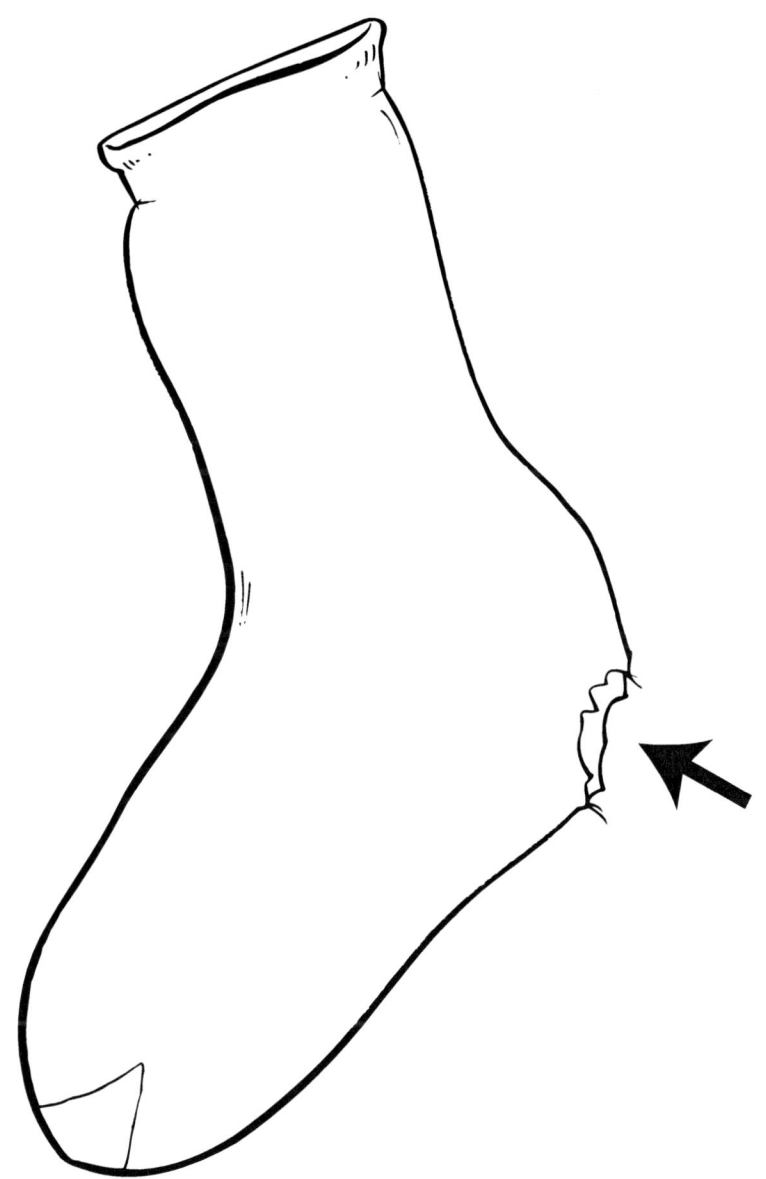

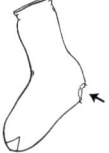

Some socks have holes!

Concept: Socks

Yes-No Questions

1. Are socks toys?
2. Are socks clothing?
3. Are two socks a pair?
4. Are three socks a pair?
5. Do socks cover your head?
6. Do socks cover your feet?
7. Do socks keep feet cool?
8. Do all socks look the same?
9. Are some socks long?
10. Do people put socks on before shoes?

Wh- and How Questions

1. Where do people wear socks?
2. How many socks are in a pair?
3. What do people put on their feet before shoes?
4. What do socks cover?
5. Who wears socks?

Socks Generalization Page

Circle the socks. Put an X on each picture that is not socks.

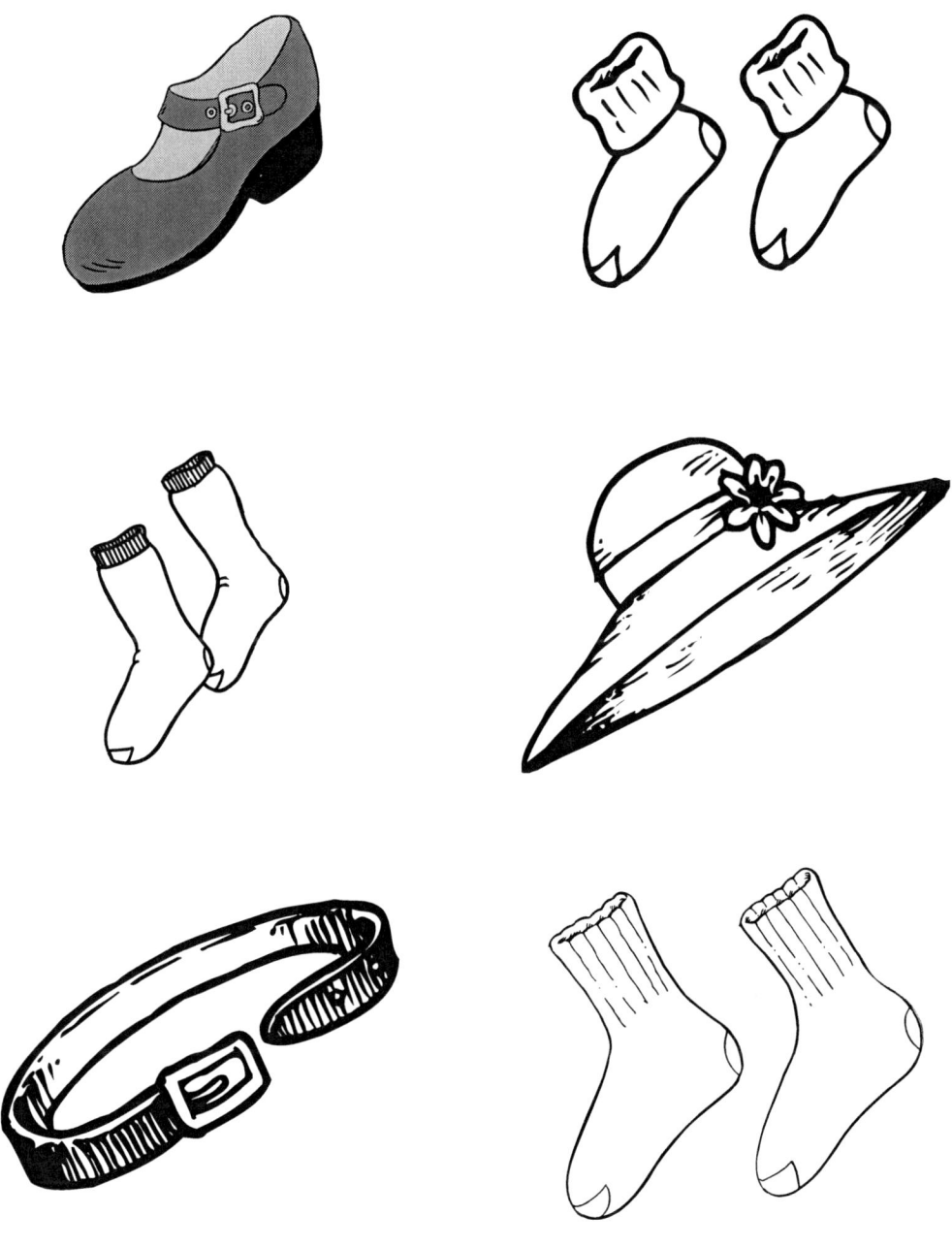

Socks
Concept Development

Socks Mini-Book

Copy this page. Cut apart the boxes on the dotted lines. Put the story in order to make a little book and staple.

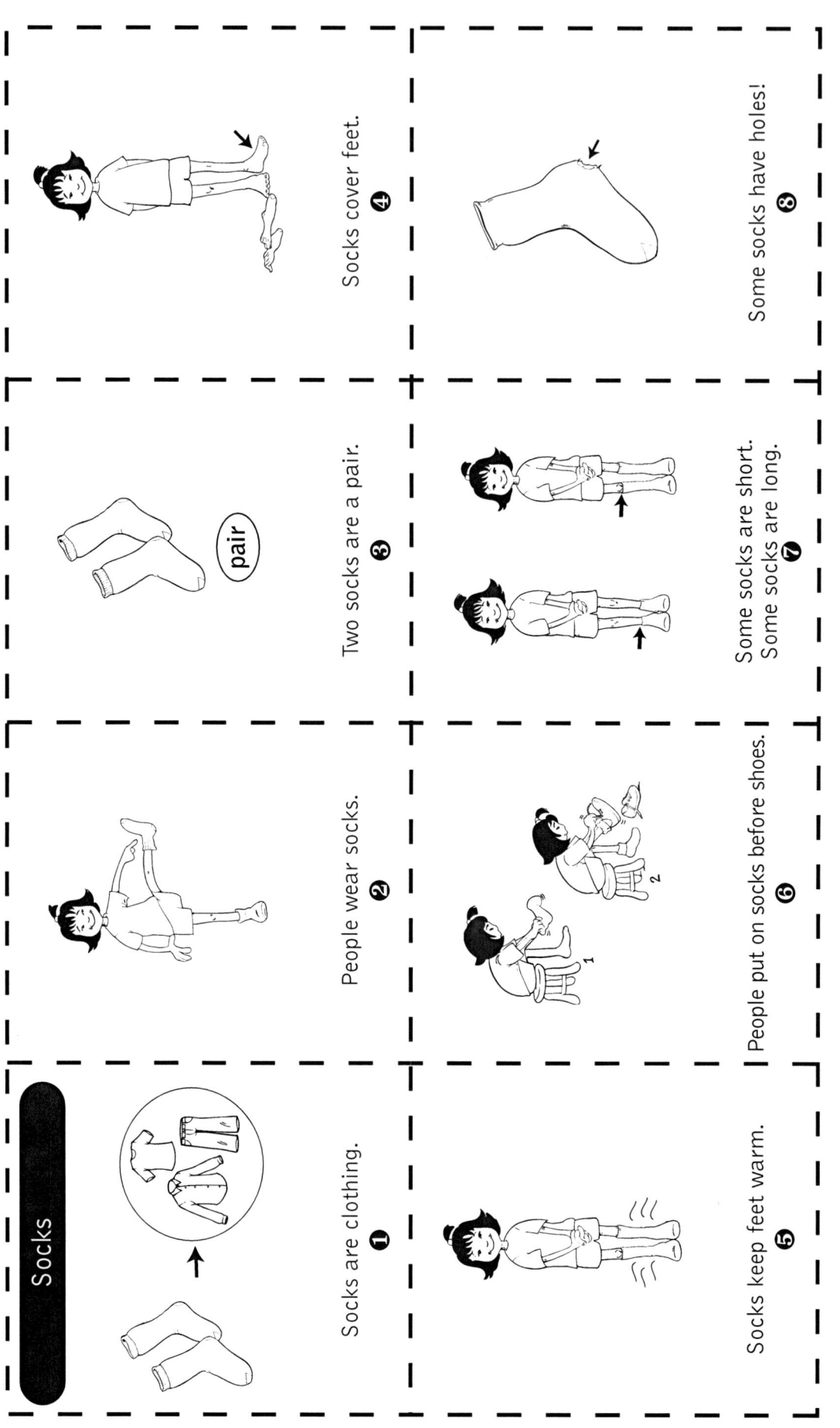

1. Socks are clothing.
2. People wear socks.
3. Two socks are a pair.
4. Socks cover feet.
5. Socks keep feet warm.
6. People put on socks before shoes.
7. Some socks are short. Some socks are long.
8. Some socks have holes!

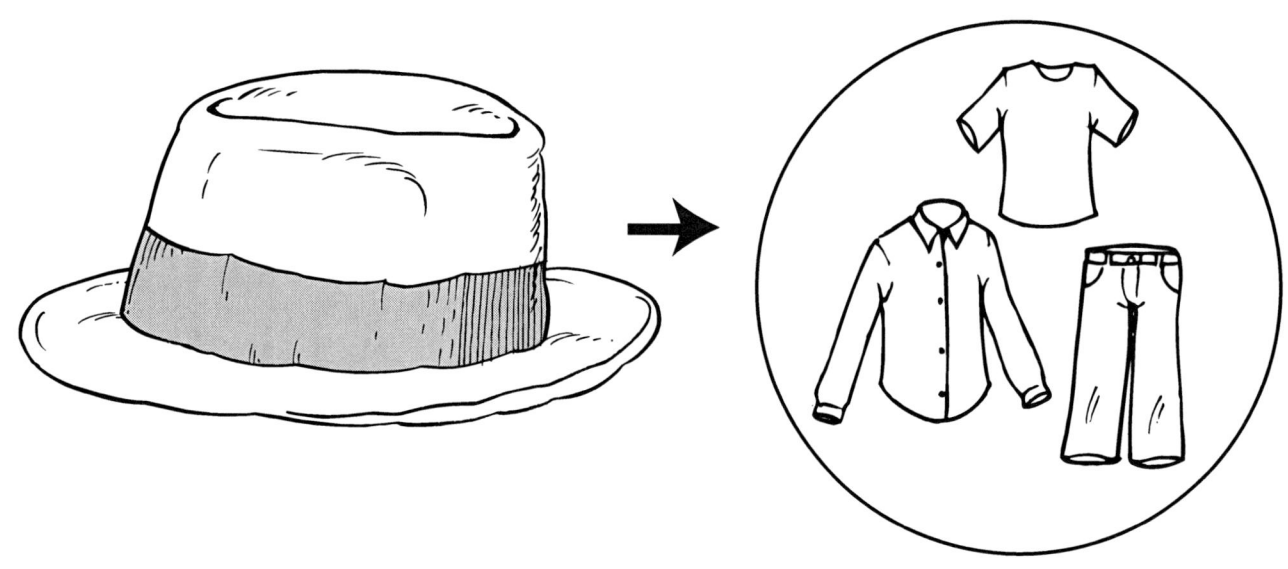

A hat is clothing.

People wear hats.

Hats cover heads.

People wear hats when it is sunny.

Hat
Concept Development

People wear hats when it is cold.

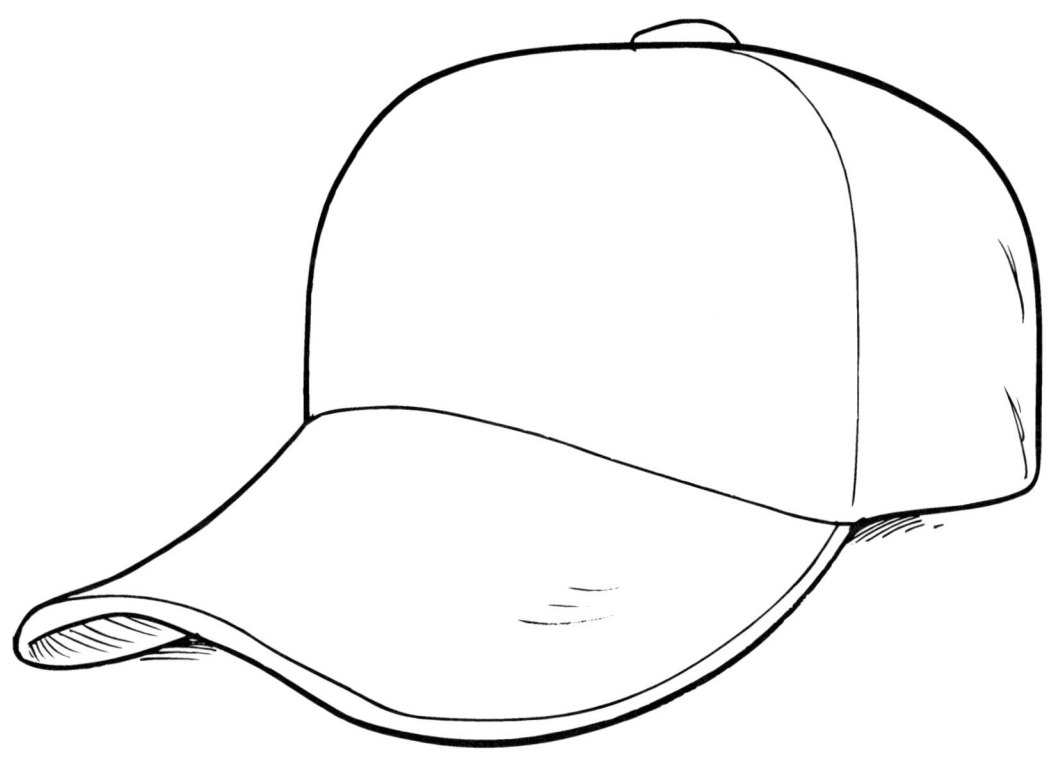

This is a cap.

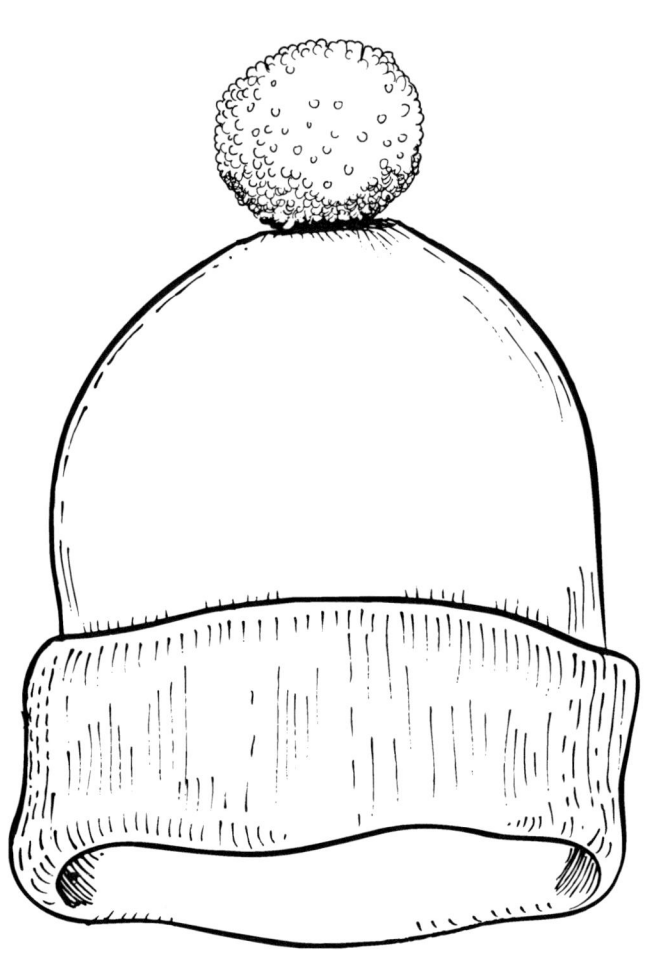

This is a stocking cap.

All of these are hats.

Concept: Hat

Yes-No Questions

1. Is a mitten a hat?
2. Do people wear hats?
3. Do hats cover arms?
4. Do hats cover heads?
5. Do all hats look the same?
6. Do people wear hats when it's sunny?
7. Is a stocking cap a car?
8. Is a cap a hat?
9. Do people wear hats when it's cold?
10. Do hats cover hair?

Wh- and How Questions

1. What do people do with hats?
2. What do hats cover?
3. Who wears hats?
4. When do people wear hats?
5. What do people wear on their heads?

Hat Generalization Page

Circle the hats. Put an X on each picture that is not a hat.

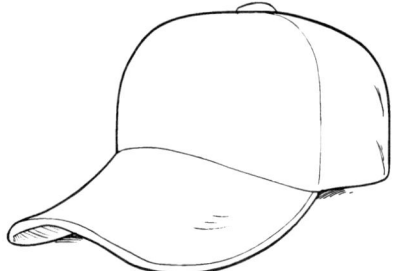
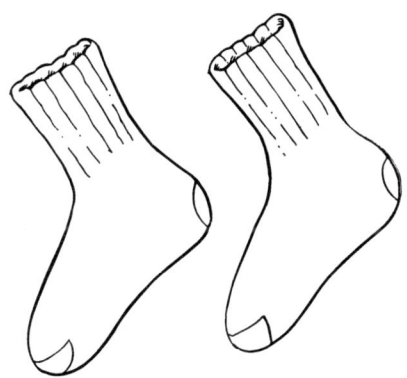
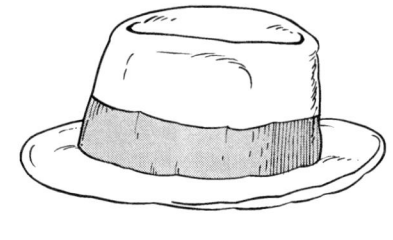
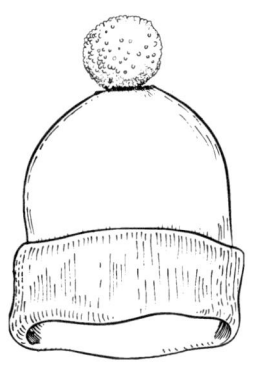

Hat Mini-Book

Copy this page. Cut apart the boxes on the dotted lines. Put the story in order to make a little book and staple.

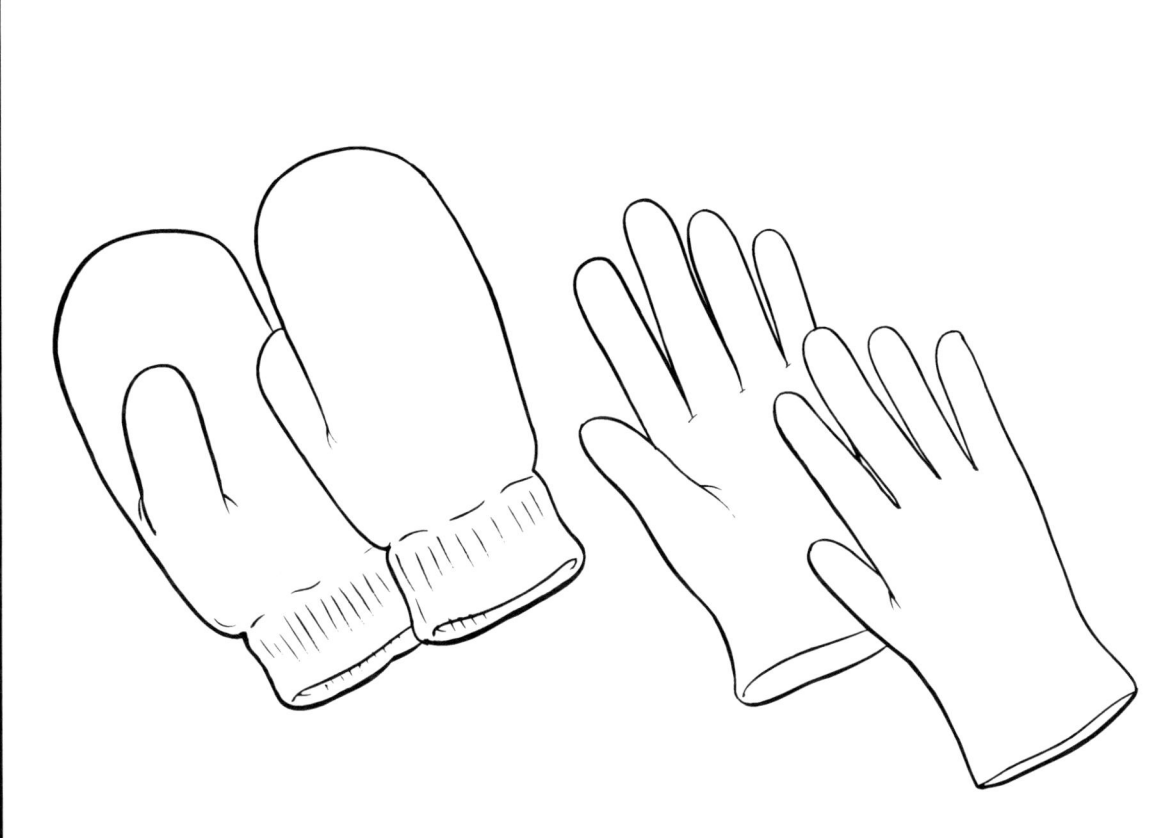

Mittens and Gloves

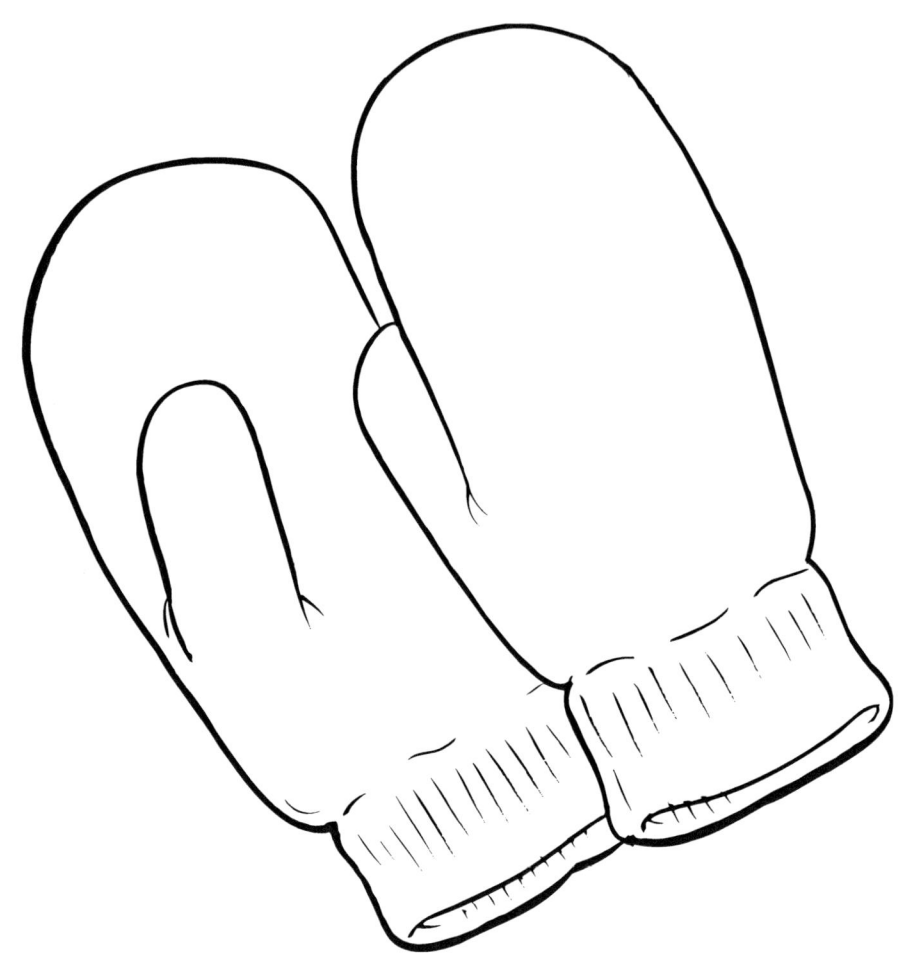

These are mittens.

These are gloves.

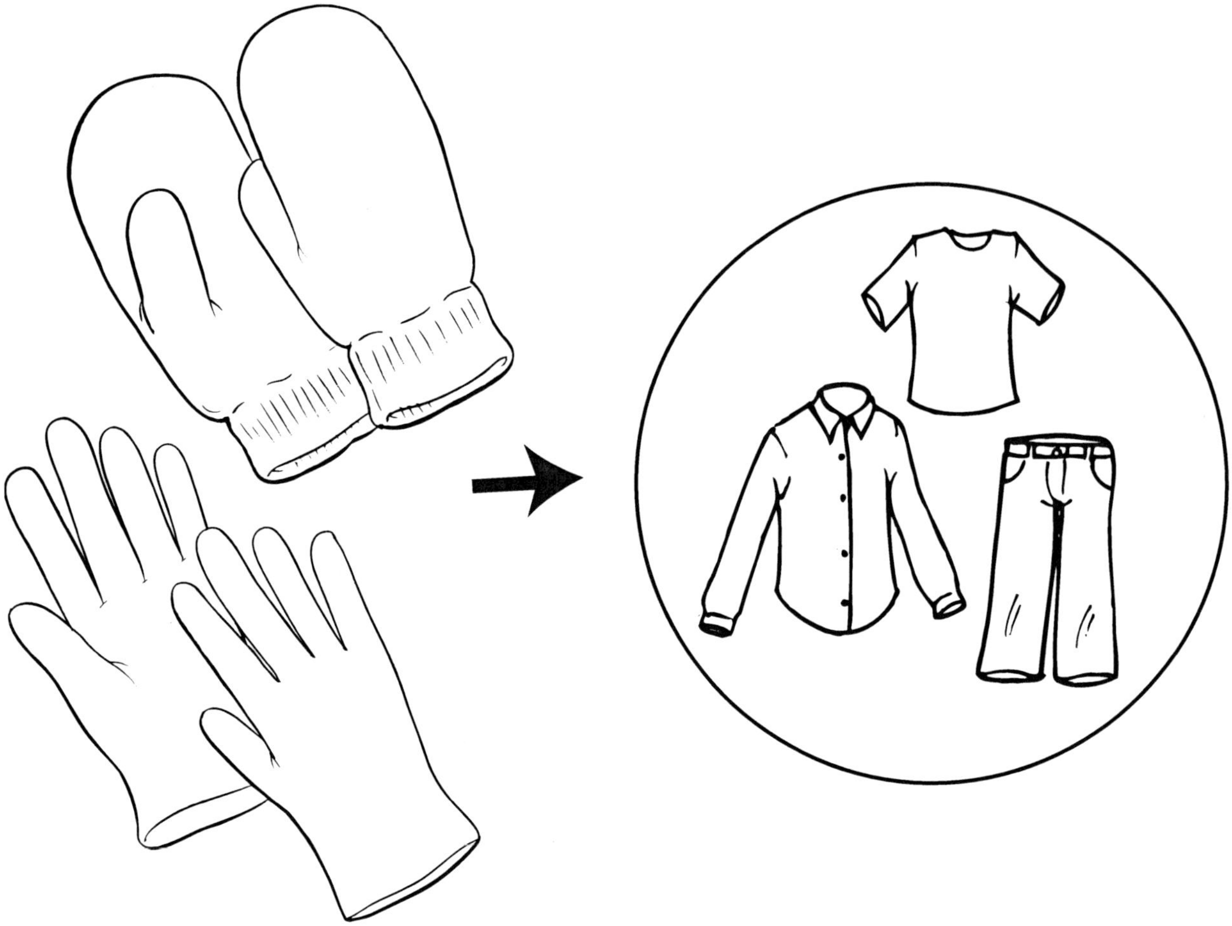

Mittens and gloves are clothing.

People wear mittens and gloves.

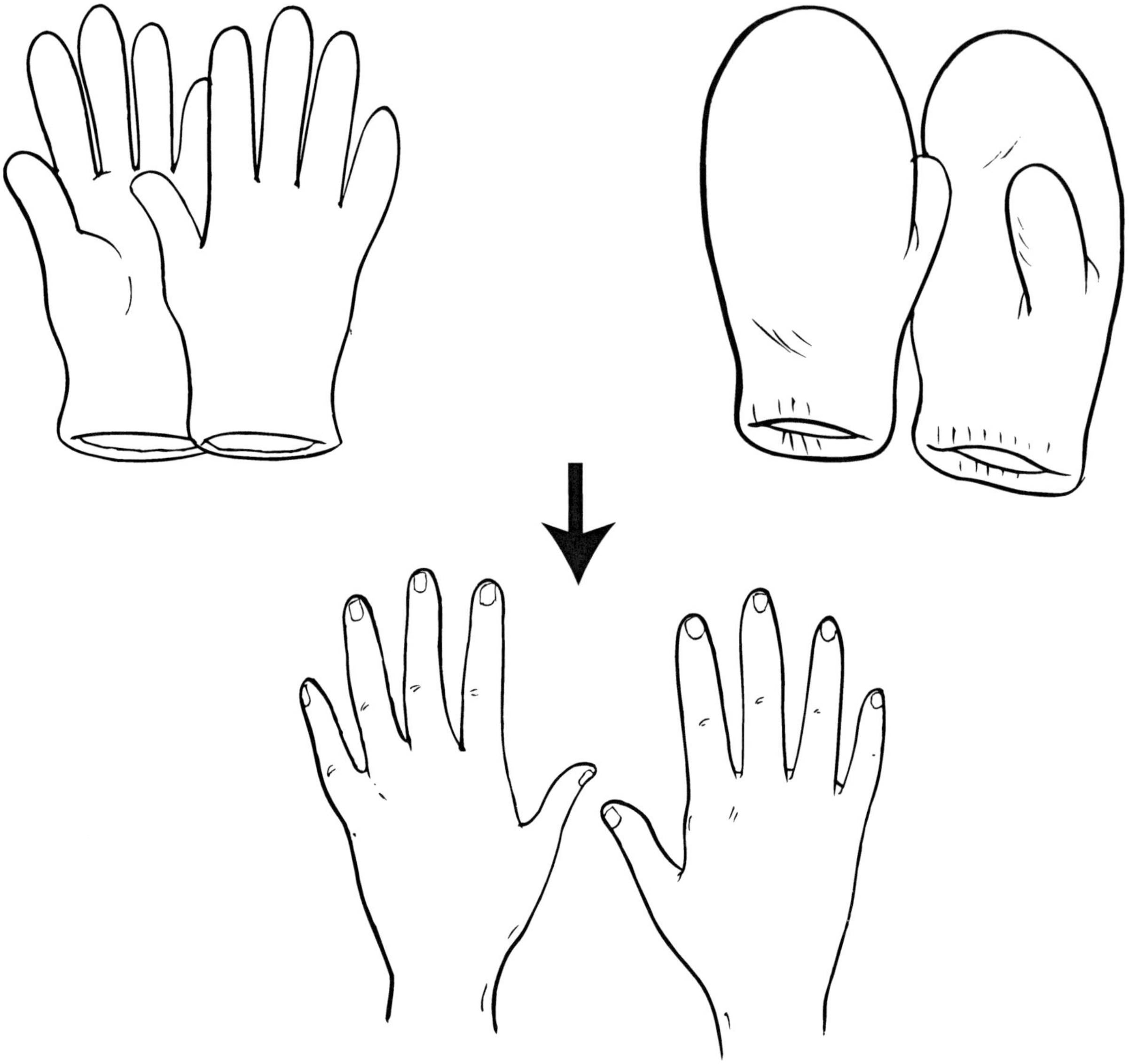

  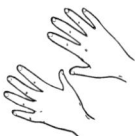

Mittens and gloves cover hands.

People wear mittens and gloves when it is cold.

  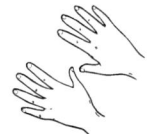 

Mittens and gloves keep hands warm.

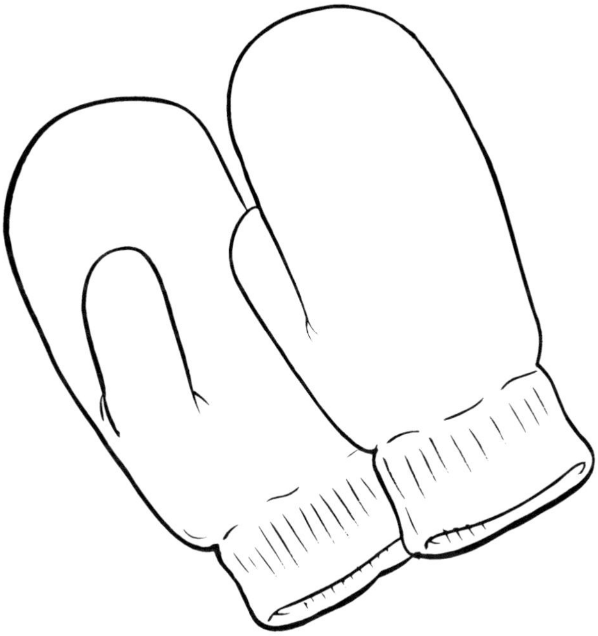

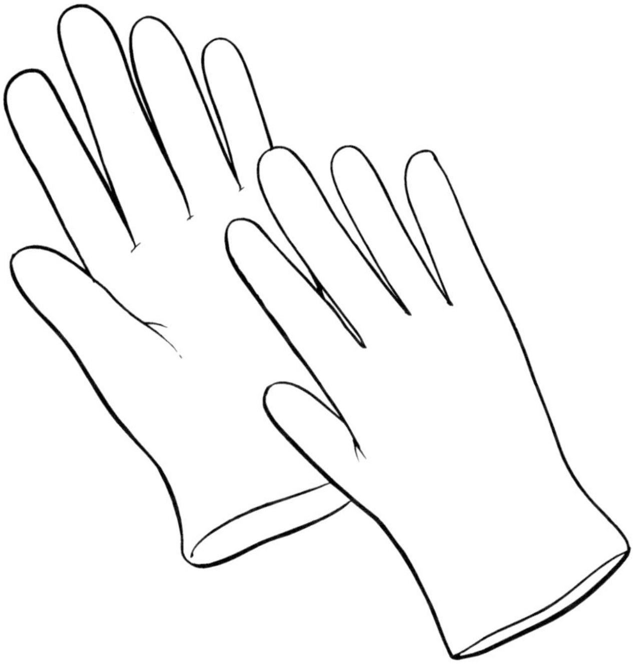

pair   pair

2     2

Two mittens or two gloves are a pair.

Concept: Mittens and Gloves

Yes-No Questions

1. Are mittens and gloves furniture?
2. Are mittens and gloves clothing?
3. Do dogs wear mittens and gloves?
4. Do people wear mittens and gloves?
5. Do mittens and gloves cover the feet?
6. Are three mittens in a pair?
7. Do people wear mittens and gloves when it's cold?
8. Do mittens and gloves keep hands warm?
9. Do mittens and gloves look the same?
10. Do mittens and gloves cover the hands?

Wh- and How Questions

1. Who wears mittens and gloves?
2. What do mittens and gloves cover?
3. How many mittens are in a pair?
4. When do people wear mittens and gloves?
5. Why do people wear mittens and gloves?

Mittens and Gloves Generalization Page

Circle the mittens and gloves. Put an X on each picture that is not mittens or gloves.

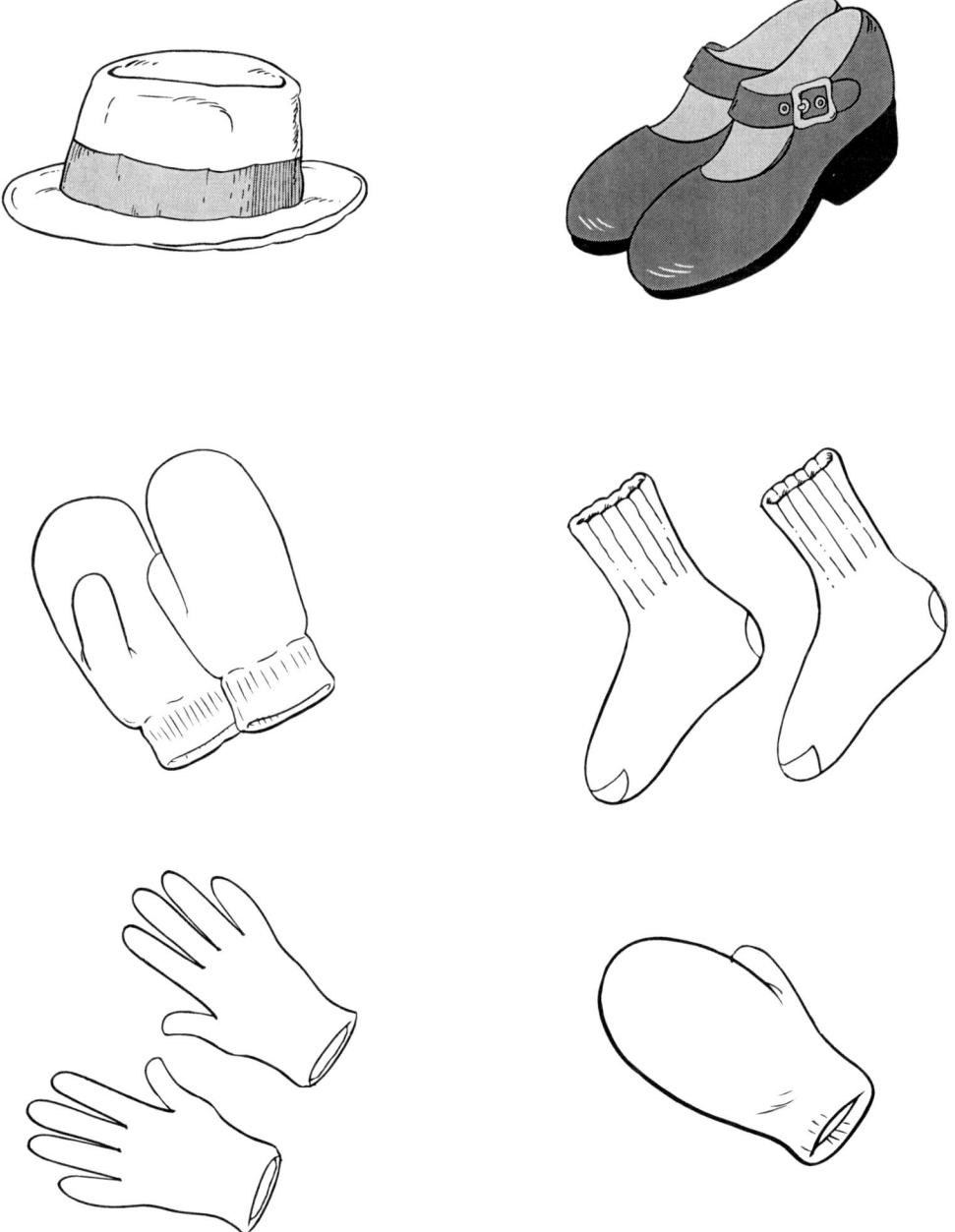

Mittens and Gloves Mini-Book

Copy this page. Cut apart the boxes on the dotted lines. Put the story in order to make a little book and staple.

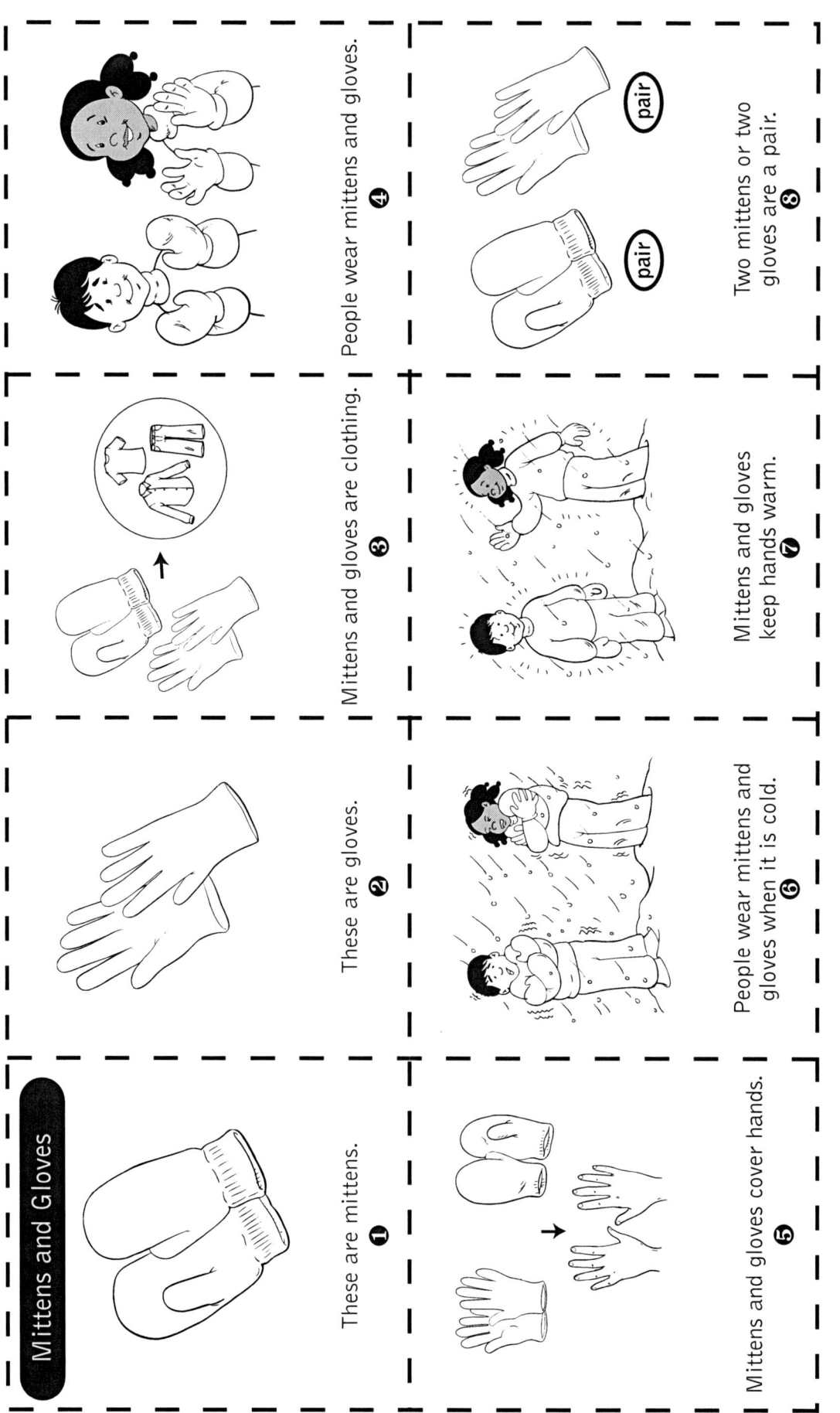

Mittens and Gloves
Concept Development

Pajamas and nightgowns are clothing.

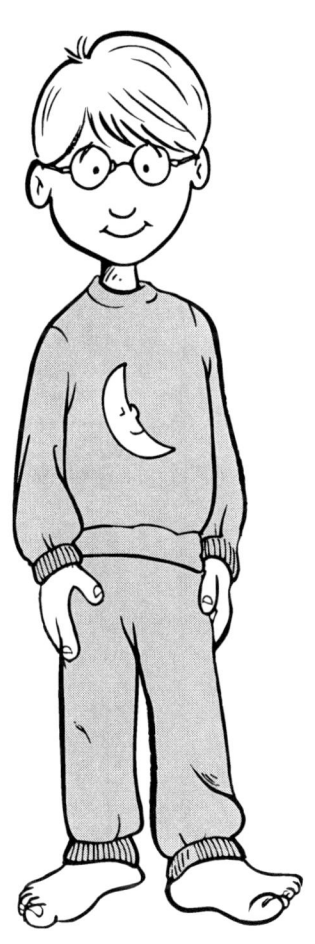

People wear pajamas and nightgowns.

People wear pajamas or nightgowns to sleep.

Sometimes people wear pajamas when they are sick.

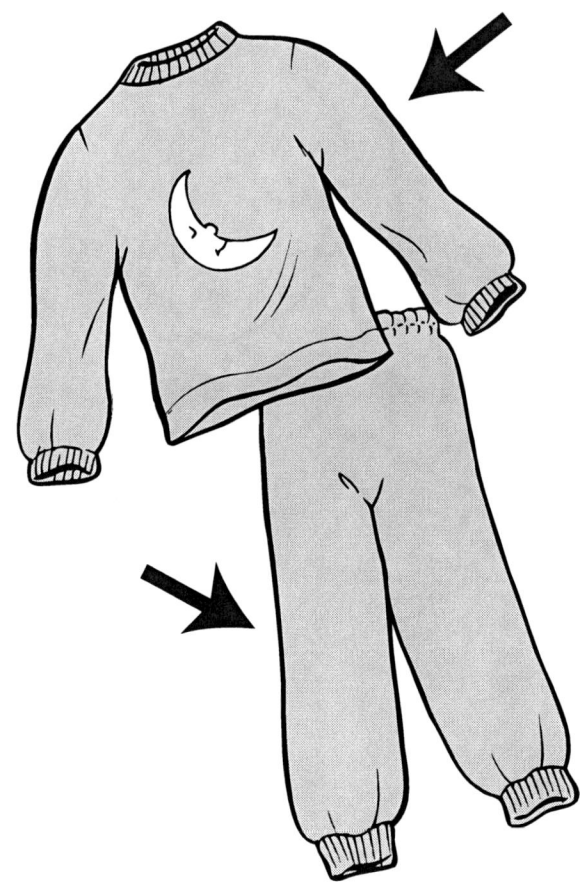

  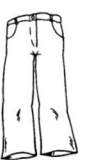

Pajamas have a shirt and pants.

Boys and girls wear pajamas.

A nightgown looks like a dress.

Only girls wear nightgowns.

Concept: Pajamas and Nightgowns

Yes-No Questions

1. Are pajamas and nightgowns toys?
2. Are pajamas and nightgowns clothing?
3. Do people wear pajamas and nightgowns?
4. Do people put on pajamas or nightgowns to play?
5. Do people put on pajamas or nightgowns to sleep?
6. Is a nightgown a dress for sleeping?
7. Can girls wear pajamas?
8. Does a nightgown have a shirt and pants?
9. Can people wear pajamas or nightgowns when they are sick?
10. Do boys wear nightgowns?

Wh- and How Questions

1. What do people do with pajamas and nightgowns?
2. When do people wear pajamas and nightgowns?
3. Who can wear pajamas?
4. Which clothing has a shirt and pants?
5. Who can wear a nightgown?

Pajamas and Nightgowns Generalization Page

Circle the pajamas and nightgowns. Put an X on each picture that is not pajamas or a nightgown.

Pajamas and Nightgowns Mini-Book

Copy this page. Cut apart the boxes on the dotted lines. Put the story in order to make a little book and staple.

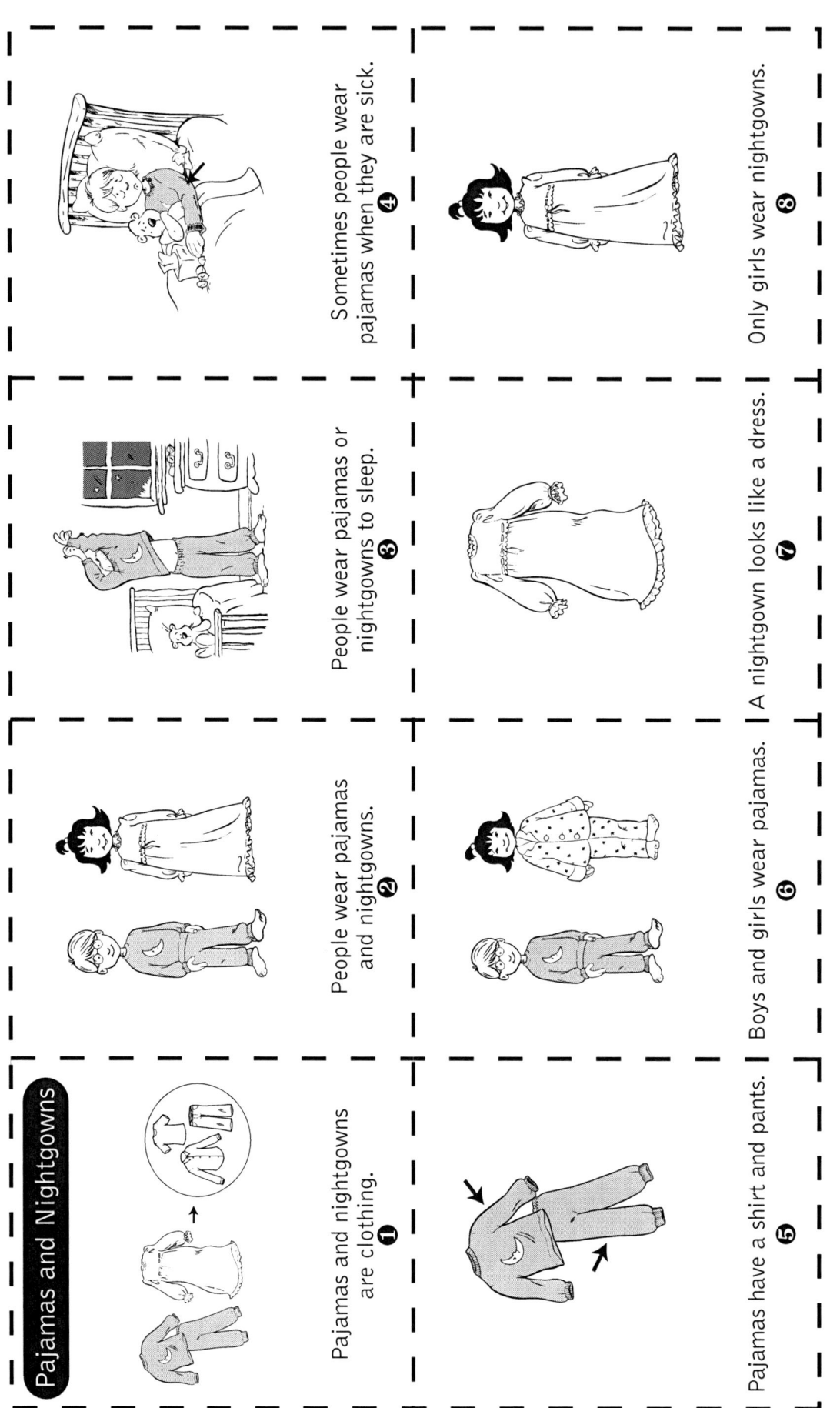

Pajamas and Nightgowns
Concept Development

Match-Up Activity

Materials: pairs of shoes, pairs of socks, pairs of mittens and gloves, a box

Copy the *same* and *different* Picture Prompt cards. Use the cards to explain each task. The cards may be helpful to redirect the child if he or she is unsuccessful in matching the items.

Step 1: Put one shoe from each pair into the box. Show one of the remaining shoes to the child. Encourage the child to search in the box for the matching shoe. Repeat this activity with socks, mittens, and gloves.

Step 2: Put several pairs of shoes into the box. Have the child take them out and pair them up. Repeat this activity with socks, mittens, and gloves.

Step 3: Put matching pairs of shoes, socks, mittens, and gloves into the box. Have the child take them out and pair them up correctly.

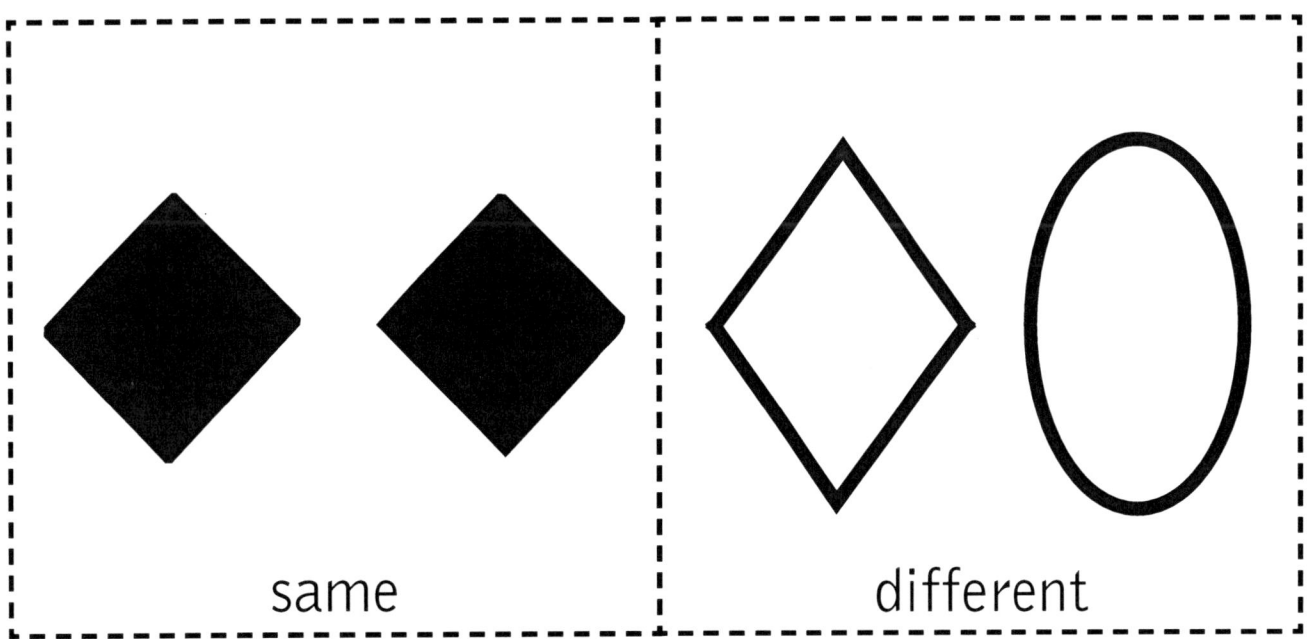

Extension Activity

Dress the boy in clothes from pages 132–134.

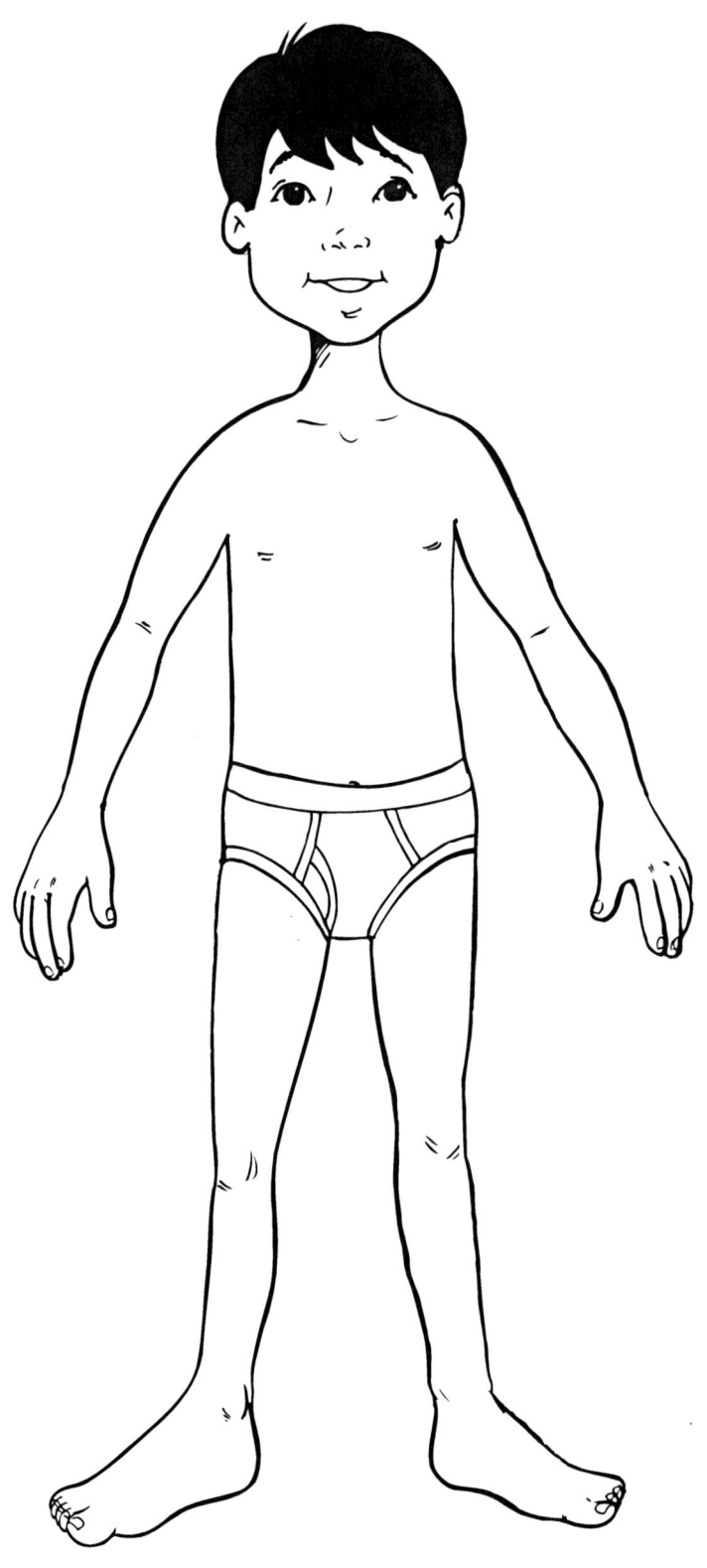

Extension Activity, continued

Dress the girl in clothes from pages 132–134.

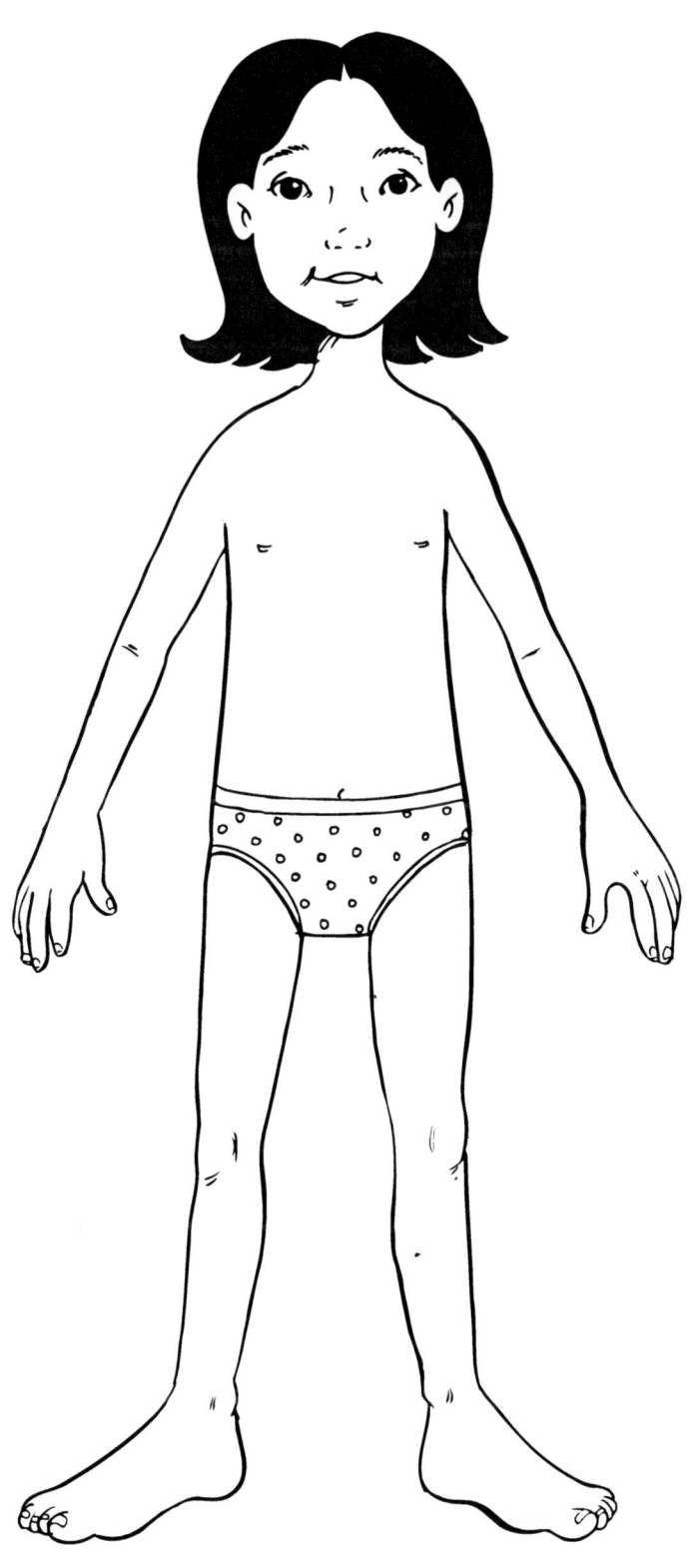

Extension Activity, continued

Cut out the clothes below and on pages 133 and 134. Use them to dress the boy on page 130 and the girl on page 131.

Extension Activity, continued

Cut out the clothes below and on pages 132 and 134. Use them to dress the boy on page 130 and the girl on page 131.

Concept Development

Extension Activity, continued

Cut out the clothes below and on pages 132 and 133. Use them to dress the boy on page 130 and the girl on page 131.

Concept Development

Suggested Literature

Clothing
New Boots For Spring: A Book of Seasons by Harriet Zeifert
The Jacket I Wear in the Snow by Shirley Neitzel
Dressing by Helen Oxenbury
Touch and Feel Clothes by DK Publishing
Baby's Clothes by Neil Ricklen
Barney's Clothes by Mary Ann Dudko
Clothes by David Brown
My Clothes by Patricia Almada

Shoes
Whose Shoes? by Rebel Williams
Shoes by Elizabeth Winthrop

Socks
A Pair of Socks by Stuart J. Murphy

Hat
Hats by Debra Lee
Hats by Sarah Wilson
Old Hat, New Hat by Stan and Jan Berenstain
Hats, Hats, Hats photographs by Ken Heyman

Pajamas and Nightgowns
Pajamas by Livingston Taylor